Heaven is Here: Our Ascent into the Fifth Dimension

By Alana Kay

Heaven is Here: Our Ascent into the Fifth Dimension

By Alana Kay
www.alanakay.com

ISBN: 978-0-972723213

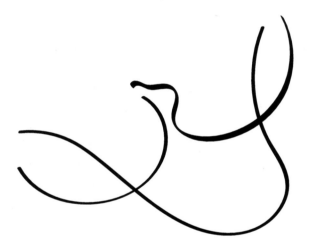

VIOLET PHOENIX PUBLISHING

P.O. Box 644
Kihei, Hawaii 96753

Table of Contents

PREFACE

These are the best of times and these are the worst of times. Your experience the next few years will depend on your perception and which plane of existence you are tuned into. A high-frequency energy has enveloped our planet to restore it to its original state. The reign of darkness is over and its debris is being flushed out. Embrace this light and it will transform your life forever. Let go of fear. It is time to ascend with Gaia.

Heaven on Earth...

The Golden Age of Enlightenment is here. Although Heaven has truly always been a part of us, it has never been as available as it is now. As a matter of fact, this energy is so prevalent; it has become a mandate. The crystal structures that hold the destiny for our planet are intact after eons of damage. This beautiful, light energy of Love is the plan for our planet and our Universe.

Sometimes referred to as the Aquarian Age or the Fifth Sun, we have entered a time period when this paradigm shift is imminent. This period of time is the gateway to ascension and we will soon be able to enjoy peace on Earth, but there is work to be done. While the energy shift is one part of the equation; we humans are the other part of the equation. We need to activate our light bodies and vibrate in a higher frequency in order to cooperate with this energy. It is up to us to go deep into our being in order to birth the changes. Change can be a bit messy, but the sooner we get through it, the better.

We need to look deeper; we need to feel deeper; we need to live with a greater sense of meaning and purpose. Without going into the depths of our being, there is no Heaven – just the temporal. The magic begins when we step into the eternal side of life.

We also need to get back to connecting with nature and the nature spirits. As we do so, we will learn how to heal our ecosphere. Each of us played a part in creating discordant energies and each of us will play a part in the healing of all of the systems – great and small.

We are the change agents, the catalysts, and

the bridge builders.

There are countless spiritual teachings in addition to countless ways of crunching the numbers, but we may begin by acknowledging that our planet has been under construction for some 4.5 billion years. The Universe as we know it has been evolving even longer than our planet. Upon studying the history of the natural development thereof, the wisdom and patience that it took to bring this amazing creation into fruition should humble even the most arrogant of souls. It is a most amazing time to be alive. While we work through some of the messes we created, we need to take the time to look at the pure splendor of this majestic planet.

In order for humanity to incarnate here, we had to arrive in organic form because this energy is continually being created and re-created. In order to work within the natural laws of Gaia, we have inhabited an animal-like body with a bit of tweaking to allow for the maximum flexibility in expression of spirit. Living as spirit beings in organic human bodies has been challenging and it has been a part of our evolution as a species.

This inherent disposition for humanity has been a struggle and we have created karma. Karma is anything that is not in accordance with God's will or God's plan for this planet. We need to forgive others and ourselves for our humanness. It has gotten pretty ugly at times and we have also become hosts for dark energies in the process. We can be done with this now. Our causal bodies, DNA and chakra systems keep all of the evolutionary information we need to reincarnate effectively each time and not repeat things. If we fix things now, we will carry the corrections into subsequent incarnations. DNA changes as we change and we pass this on to future generations.

We are at the end of a karmic cycle, so it follows that it is time to clear up our karma before we move into the new cycle. In addition to clearing up our karma, we are dealing with dark forces and trickster energies, which will require us to learn how to read and deal with subtle energies in a very efficient way. Many who attempt to rise find that dark forces will try to impede their success. Persistence is tantamount to breaking through. We must cease becoming victims of the fear mongers. Many dramas are playing out as we become aware of that which needs to leave our collective consciousness.

While there is debate over how long we as humans have been evolving here, it has not been long in comparison to the big picture. Some say it has been 26,000-years and others say it is more or less. Actually, it is more likely that human like beings have evolved and devolved during varying periods throughout time. During this time period, we can apply what we have learned and correct our course with accumulated wisdom.

The human creative cycle and integration period have come to a point where we have to rapidly clear up our past and align with our true nature.

As Earth has evolved, we as expressions of God have also evolved through time. We have evolved physically, mentally, emotionally and spiritually. Our technology has evolved to the point where we don't have to put as much of our energy into survival as we did in prior times. Although it may not appear at times to be the case, we are finally at Heaven's door, the overwhelming majority of humans ready to move into a new paradigm of peace and Love. It is going to get easier to live here as we move on.

We may refer to the new energy as the Golden Age, the Aquarian Age, the Fifth Dimension, or the Fifth Sun.

We need to learn how to live together in the state of peace and Love. In 1 John 4:16, The Holy Bible says: ..."God is Love. Whoever lives in Love lives in God, and God in Him."

Some people see Love as a weakness, but indeed it is the greatest strength on Earth. In its unadulterated state, Love is the only power that has the wisdom to create, heal, and restore lasting change to any person, place or thing. This fact will be demonstrated over time. As we embrace Love and its facets, we learn how to create with Love. We cannot blame our way back into integrity – we must Love our way back.

In essence, *Heaven is Here*, is a book about Love – not the kind of Love we equate with adoration, attraction or desire, but the ever-prevalent dimension or vibration of Love that has been talked about by spiritual masters throughout history. It is about Love of self, service, humanity, the natural world and spirit or God. The God force, being the frequency of Love, has many facets and it is what we have been evolving into over the past creative cycle. We have been learning how to be co-creators with this frequency. We have learned through trial and error. Our planet has gone through some major attacks by the darkness and it has been saved over and over again.

It is time to forgive and put the past behind us. We don't want to have distain for humans; we just need to learn to be better humans. We need to be supportive of each other through this process.

Love is The Creative Force- a parallel dimension,

accessible to all.

Living in the state of Love, or with the heart, creates the experience of Heaven on Earth and is basically uncharted territory for humans in part because we have been patiently creating the physical world in which we live – causing us to have more mental focus than heart centered focus. As a result, we have learned to value logic over instincts. Because a dedication to the spiritual realm of life reveals an entirely different vision and requires an entirely different set of tools than those we used in the material realm, navigating the waters can be scary to some who don't know the brilliant caverns this dimension will lead you through. It is easy to feel like we are losing control when we lighten up.

We are also out of balance. The world has been awash with male domination. This was part of our evolution, but now it is time to temper this energy with the feminine once again. Sheer male energy that is not balanced has created a culture of competition and fear. There is hope, because the younger generation is coming in much more balanced. The darkness has been able to collaborate with this male energy and has all but extinguished the divine feminine. As women reclaim their power and men learn how to work with the female instead of over powering or dismantling this aspect, we will create a new paradigm of balanced creative energies and the result will be phenomenal.

Harnessing the power within by embracing a heart-centered life will return health, energy, vitality, and true wisdom to the spiritual seeker. We don't have to be sick and tired anymore. Many have touched on this realm and then turned away because it is unfamiliar. Admittedly, it is difficult to know how we are doing when we let go of society's markers of success.

Many have turned back because spiritual growth requires us to go through some voids before we transform and that can be scary to some people. Also, when we open up our minds and our energy, we find that there are more things to manage. Unfortunately, we must go through this phase of awkwardness in order to get to the other side. Take heart because we are all in this together and there are many spiritual teachers who will assure you as you go that there is truly a better life in store for those who will let go of the old ways.

Learning to live a heart centered life can make us feel like a child again – having to learn many new things.

I have dedicated my life to exploring the deeper dimensions, especially since 1994 and although I have had some difficulty at times, I have found it to be the only truly useful endeavor I have embarked on largely because it continually builds upon itself, revealing more and more as I go. I discovered access to creativity and wisdom as well as renewed energy and joy as I went. It is the ultimate sustainable life style. Instead of getting attached to a job, a home or a group of people, we learn to connect to our soul or Source energy. Source energy provides us with constant wisdom, energy and freedom.

We are all experiencing acceleration and it can be confusing. It is important to stop abusing ourselves on all levels and treat each moment and each experience as though it is precious. We must take time to review our lives every day.

My motivation in writing *Heaven is Here*, is to give those who have always been intrigued with the etheric realms, or felt the power of a loving heart, the permission, the wherewithal and the support to come out of the closet and take the time to develop the power within, learn how to use it to heal yourself and make the world a better place for everyone. For those who are still in resistance, the pressure can seem unbearable.

Heaven is Here is meant to be a practical outline, while supporting time honored spiritual teachings and weaving them together in such a way that spiritual seekers of all levels may find a journey that will be purposeful and exciting. I see the need to fill in some of the blanks and provide encouragement and also to dispel some of the myths that surround the dynamics of this time in our evolution.

I desire to help people find the way to become experts at receiving the answers themselves while feeling good-about their lives on planet Earth. When we are empowered and connected to our inner being, we do not give in to fear and deception because we are sure of the power of the spirit and our inner wisdom.

Blessed are the meek (gentle), for they shall inherit

the Earth... Matthew 5:5

If you have ever wondered what the words, the meek shall inherit the earth mean or have had a strong feeling that there is great change afoot, you are likely to see these concepts playing out in front of you more as time goes on. We are already witnessing the weakening of great institutions and people in positions of power at this time. The so-called meek are in position to take over. Humanity is waking up. Don't deny the glimpses you may have into your role in the awakening. We are experiencing the upwelling of the voice of God and our inner voices are becoming louder and stronger all the time.

Our planet and its inhabitants will no longer tolerate the imbalances of the lower energies. The great energetic changes we are experiencing are the primary cause of the turmoil and confusion that we are experiencing globally, nationally and personally. We mustn't hold on to the chaotic images too long, lest we create more karma and pain for ourselves. As all of the darkness appears, we must transform it and move on and fill the void with a more beautiful vision. All may not appear heavenly at times, but take heart that everything is headed in the right direction and things are transforming as certainly as the sun comes up each day.

Even racial tensions that we thought were behind us are coming up again for review. This is how it works. We keep running through things until we resolve them completely.

Any discomfort that we feel is the higher energies
clearing the older energies out.

The power has shifted on the planet from the ego to the spirit and only those who know how to surrender and align with their soul will sail through the next few years with ease. We need to open up our minds as we receive an entirely new life of ease and joy.

These energetic upheavals are causing people to feel uneasy as existing foundations are shaken. Fear can cause people to conjure up some pretty good stories. If you are concerned about apocalyptic predictions, raptures and the like, it would be best to ask the light to show you what the real plan is. Don't be fooled.

I hope to help you become very confident in your sense of inner strength and your ability to discern the truth. I hope you will find useful tools to help you gain insight that will help to clarify these topics and many others so that you are not thrown off course by things. As you move through your journey, you will tap into your inner guidance and it will teach you well and reveal truths about the larger picture that you may not have considered before. When all else fails, remember the answer is always Love.

No matter where we are or what we are faced with, we always have our inner light to guide us.

This is not a time to be afraid – this is a time to be excited. Furthermore, if you are wondering what your role is and would like to be able to better navigate the turbulent energies that are prevalent at this time, I hope to help you to become clear enough in your own guidance so that you may become one of the light bringers of this golden age of consciousness. Joy activates and feeds our power centers.

Love, which has often been mistaken as a weakness, will instead rise as a power and take over the Earth in the coming years.

Those who do not get a spiritual education and shift to those power centers instead of being driven by ego will experience varying levels of difficulty because they will remain caught up in the building storm clouds of hatred, doubt and fear. There is a good chance that things could get pretty rough and will challenge us to the core. We must learn to recognize the features of the darkness and its trickery and also learn the power of the spirit and the way it behaves. Through the process of learning to discern and chose, we shed the ego and clean up our baggage, becoming much lighter and more able to function in the new energy. The challenges of this time period will help us learn to focus on our inner light.

We are here on Earth to be joyfully productive. We are meant to be working harmoniously with each other as well as the natural world. From now on, that dream is going to be easier than ever to achieve in large part because the energy supports it.

How do we make our individual contribution?

The expression, follow your heart or your instincts, is used often. What does it mean to follow your heart? Is it the same as surrendering? Is your heart the same as your soul? Why does this concept sound so simple, yet we so often find it difficult to assimilate into daily life?

When we surrender, we are not giving over our power to someone or something else, we are letting go of the self that only knows the past and opening up to the self that will show us what the possibilities for us are if we just get out of the way and let it flourish. We will be pushed to surrender much of our old ways in the coming years. All humans are capable of brilliance, but not all are tuned in.

Humans are extremely complex and the things they taught us in school will only get us so far. The things you will find in *Heaven is Here* are things that they did not teach us in school and our parents did not know any better either. We are just now beginning to understand the power of the spiritual realms largely because the veil is thinning. The seeming wall between spirit and ego is becoming transparent. This thinning is a part of the energetic changes that we are experiencing.

We are experiencing more psychic phenomenon, more synchronicity and serendipity, causing people to be more motivated than ever to get a metaphysical education. This acceleration can really cause our nerves to fray and make us feel a bit crazy. We may also be in more pain than ever before. The pain and distress is simply showing us what must be healed. Our angels and guides are ready and waiting to help us. They will help us when we open our minds and our hearts and allow the new ways to come in. This state is only temporary as we learn to integrate the new energy and step up our own game. We must be patient while we go through the process of shifting.

Let go of the fear of the unknown.

The spiritual realms and inner wisdom are not scary things. Letting go of what we are familiar with will need to become a new habit as we re-create our lives and our planet. Because certain groups throughout history have wanted to suppress others for their own benefit, we were taught to think that our inner guidance as anything from untrustworthy to evil! It is time to dispose of that thinking and begin to embrace and understand it instead. In *Heaven is Here*, I help take the mystery out of all of it for you, giving you answers and ideas you may have never heard before, revealing your instinctive center as your light in the darkness – your strength.

Ideally, a spiritual quest not only connects us with our guiding light or the God force within, revealing inner peace, joy and the answers to life's perplexing questions; it is ultimately meant to become a fulfilling lifestyle. A life aligned with the soul or heart of the self is the only thing that will forestall addictions, create satisfaction and inner peace, replace bad relationships and assure lasting, sustainable success in all things.

Heaven on Earth is a choice.

Approximately twenty years ago, a person with whom I was only vaguely familiar, began asking me some probing questions about my beliefs. At one point, she flatly asked me: "Where is Heaven?" My thoughts stopped and something inside of me clicked as I turned around to look directly at her and she said, "It's right here." Suddenly, the room got brighter and I felt different. There was definitely a shift in my consciousness. This was only the beginning of my return.

I flashed back to a moment in my youth when I read the Bible phrase, "One day heaven and Earth will be as one." The moment I was told, "It's right here," I realized that the time was now and that Heaven was mine for the asking. I set out over the next few years to discover how to live the experience of Heaven on Earth. This conversation, in conjunction with other related occurrences at that time arrived in a cluster and I began to experience what is known as acceleration. People often experience this phenomenon when they have a near death experience or other trauma. The inflow of information to me at that time was unstoppable.

Harmonic Convergence occurred in 1987,

creating a state where the Fifth Dimension is

available to all of humanity.

As I delved deeper into my spiritual identity and learned again to be instinctive and intuitive, my previously prevalent mental confusion, fogginess and fatigue became a thing of the past. Yet, I knew I still had so much more to learn and so much more to experience. A spiritual trek is a continual process, yet very rewarding as well. It is much like getting a college degree, following the curriculum of the spirit. There is no better time than now to return to our intuitive roots and begin to embrace the concept of Heaven on Earth. If you have tried before and failed, I suggest you give it a go once more and do it with all of your heart and soul. When you loose sight of your goal, remember that you simply have been duped by negative thinking and get right back on the horse.

When enough people become spirit-minded, the whole plane will be restored, but we can only take responsibility for our individual path.

The challenge to stay grounded and connected to normal every- day life on planet Earth while consuming an intense, spiritually driven curriculum was challenging, but I found a great deal of help in books written by other spiritual teachers. The later part of the 20th century and the first part of the 21st century spawned a priceless wealth of literature to support those who were beginning to open up to greater possibilities. This proliferation of authors and useful literature is indicative of our paradigm shift. These authors echoed things that I had discovered, confirming my trek as well as giving me insight into matters that I needed clarity on. For this, I owe a debt of gratitude. Because I support the literature of these great authors and don't feel the need to duplicate their efforts, I will provide a list of suggested reading at the end of each chapter.

You will notice that I integrate many different spiritual avenues and reference varying viewpoints. I use many different words to describe God, spirit, energy, and soul. This is intentional, as I believe that all have something to contribute to the formula. I have chosen the ones that have stood out in my life. I encourage everyone to choose those teachings and references that resonate with them and also encourage everyone to be gracious and accepting of other's choices of reference. We are all headed in the same direction.

You will also notice that I capitalize words that make reference to anything that is part of the God Force because my inner guidance tells me to do so.

This is not the end of the world; it is the end of the world, as we know it.

Heaven is Here is really the culmination of my life's work. I don't have a PhD or any super colossal life experience or apparition to share. I simply have a lifetime of study and pioneering in the spiritual realms – much of which has gone on behind closed doors, so to speak. I also have a soul history with the eternal priesthood of Melchezedek, which means that I have been involved in the teaching of esoteric knowledge throughout all of my incarnations. I have also been in close communication with the Ascended Masters as I have grown and evolved. The wisdom of the Masters is priceless and incredibly accurate.

As I have been an intuitive guide for a couple decades, I have come to realize that there are countless people who have touched on things of the other side, but have been scared or simply did not have the time or tools to deal with it. Despite the fact that I have had an evolutionary path that would seem to give me an advantage, I was born just like all others, into families who were dealing with their own karma and I had karma and contracts as well to resolve.

I have spent countless hours becoming adept at navigating even the darkest corridors of life with a bright light. I have pushed all of my limits and stood on the edge of the cliff and took leaps of faith time and time again. There are times when the ascension spiral can become scary. There are times when we feel like we are in a void – but we must walk through it.

I reach out to those who find themselves grappling with the dilemma of feeling stuck in a mundane life and wanting something more, but encountering trepidation over the handling of day to day survival and the difficulty of personal relationships. I feel the need to help those hopeful people expand their horizons, especially now, in light of the higher energies that are enveloping our planet. We mustn't be too hard on ourselves – the pressures and responsibilities of life are plenty to cope with.

I also reach out to those who find themselves feeling like the lone ranger – lost in the sea of humanity. We don't have to be society dropouts, turn to drugs and alcohol or live in a monastery in order to cope with our humanity. Wake up and look around you. People are becoming more aware. Besides, it is our duty to bridge the gap, so bridge we must.

As I integrated the practical application of spiritual teachings, I discovered that I could maintain the Heaven within while navigating the chaos.

The darkness would have us give up on believing that we can make the world a better place. I will not give up on Love nor disengage myself from the things of the spirit world even though the dimension can seem elusive when confronted with the challenges of modern day living. I Love this planet and I Love my life here, so I continually refine my ability to straddle both worlds – enjoying and doing well in both. I don't let human drama interfere with my ability to enjoy a joyful, fruitful life. Some have died trying. Let's be more understanding of others and ourselves so we can walk through this doorway of evolution.

Recommended Viewing: YouTube Video: Hidden Human History Story (reflects on the teachings of Drunvalo Melchezedek)

WISHING ON YOUR OWN STAR

Whenever I look out on the nighttime sky, I become completely enraptured with the power and beauty of the stars. I have often found the starlight to be one of the most centering and powerful forces available when I need clarity. It is said that each star is the dwelling place of the individual units of consciousness or the storehouse for our causal body's energy. I believe this to be true and I am sure that this is why we are so enamored with stars. It is as though we are reminded of the magnanimity of life in its purest state when we gaze up at them. It also helps to put the little things back into the proper perspective.

Just as the starlight endures, the consciousness that dwells within all of us has always been and will never cease to exist. Beginnings and endings are part of the physical world, which has been co-created with this same energy. The Love and life that we feel inside our hearts goes with us into any dimension we enter. It is our soul that directs our undertakings and the physical body is simply a vehicle or a temporary disposition.

This consciousness, which may be referred to as our over-soul or higher self, has been through an evolution that is for the most part, something that we cannot accurately fathom and this is probably the main reason that we often do not remember too much from our past lives. Some believe that our individual units of consciousness were involved in the creation of our planet and that we have incarnated as beings other than human throughout Earth's evolution, seeing it through the many phases it has gone through to come to fruition as a life supporting planet. We needed to participate in the successful completion of our planet before we could begin our human evolution. Although it does not always seem like it, there is a reason for all of our lives and all of the drama throughout human history.

Even the simplest of esoteric belief systems acknowledge that we have had at least several incarnations as a human being. Some believe we have had tens of thousands of incarnations, while A Course in Miracles states that there aren't really past lives because there is only this moment in time. I realize that in the truest sense, our I AM presence is the only true presence, but for the purpose of working with energy and clearing programming, it may be necessary to take past life experiences into account. Now that is some serious food for thought!

Regardless of our beliefs, spirit makes sure that we know everything we need to know for this lifetime as long as we are open to it. I mention the subject because it helps to open this door should some out of the ordinary things occur.

As we move through life and our evolutionary spiral, our higher self makes sure we have everything we need and every thing we need to know.

I don't believe we have to intimately understand the grandeur and history of our soul, but we do need to have a healthy respect for it as well as a general overview of its blueprint, since we all bring our special imprint to the table and should honor and cherish those aspects. Most of us are aware from a young age what our particular talents and likes and dislikes are. It is important to be familiar with our soul lineage because it serves as our support system on the other side. As we get more famil-iar with our particular contribution and the wisdom we have accumulated throughout our individual evolution, we then learn how to apply it to this lifetime, in this body, on planet Earth.

Our higher self is that part of our identity that is really in charge of things in our lives and it knows quite a bit more than our earthly selves. It knows our history both in this lifetime as well as our previous lifetimes. It knows and understands the goals that were set forth upon our current incarnation. For most of us, there are many roads we need to walk down and many choices to make along the way. For these reasons, it is wise to learn to let it lead us. Surrendering to our soul is a practiced discipline. We surrender and feel the flow and then we get off track again. It is up to us to continually make the right choices.

We could think of our soul as an external hard drive.

Our higher self is the voice of wisdom that speaks to us as well as the creator of the visions we receive. When we talk about surrender, this is what we mean – we surrender to our higher self instead of letting our small self lead the way. If we learn to allow our higher self to lead us, step by step, it is impossible to go astray. Our soul is always one step ahead of us, but does not always follow a predictable or straight pathway, like the one our logical mind seeks. As we learn to trust this energy, we develop what is known as faith. We let go of the toiling of the ego mind and feel our gentle, powerful soul go out before us. There is great peace in the feeling of being protected and led by our Source energy.

We need to slow down in order to be led by our soul.

Although we are here to have a good time, we are also

here to take on certain challenges and we will be guided to learn much. Very often, we are involved in something that our ego is judging as yucky, yet our over-soul knows that it is for our own good. Whenever we find our thoughts and feelings bouncing around, sometimes being entirely contradictory – it is most likely that we are volleying between our heart and our head as well as many other forces. In time we learn who the winner is. We actually move more quickly through seeming difficulties if we surrender to the moment and do our best and then some.

Our full over-soul/higher self has much too much energy to fit into our physical body and this too varies by individual. While we long for our purpose, we also long for our soul's energy. Almost all cravings are the ego's yearning for union with the energy of the soul. There are stories of those who had near death experiences and whence rejoining with the larger self, a part of them did not want to return to their relatively mundane earthly existences. To their dismay, a force pushed them back into their earthbound body because they were not finished. It is the soul of the individual and the Angel guides that are responsible for this push back into the physical body because they know that the individual journey is not complete. The physical and spiritual bodies have a mutual need for each other and are designed to function together in lock step. It is critical to become acutely aware of how all of our bodies feel, so that we become adept at fine-tuning our alignment. We should know what alignment feels like even if it eludes us.

While a part of us yearns for the other side, our carnal being clings desperately to physical life by grand design because this instinct protects us from being lackadaisical about our existence here. Without this mechanism, we would likely become complacent. The cycle of death, integration and incarnation is a long and detailed process and the larger part of our selves knows that it is true! We get impatient waiting in line at the grocery store; imagine how spirit feels about us having to recycle in order to complete soul goals. Premature death short circuits the evolutionary path of the soul and is also the reason that murder and suicide are such big karmic no no's.

Spiritual disciplines, spiritual practices and self-counseling help to quell the physical aspects of our being.

Although the bliss we experience upon rejoining with the energy of the other side is alluring, extremely comfortable levels of bliss may be obtained on Earth as well if we learn how to maintain the state of being fully integrated with our spirit. Getting to know this energy that resides in us is a multi-faceted endeavor that begins by beginning to honor our instincts and feelings. We do this primarily by tuning into our instincts and acting thereupon. The more we expose ourselves to our soul, the more familiar it becomes. The only reason that we don't feel bliss is that we have lost our connection.

Our physical body only feels good when it is energetically clear and connected to our soul source energy.

We should feel healthy, energetically brilliant and deeply content at all times. This would be the case if we had all of our cosmic energy flowing through our bodies at all times. I know this sounds like a very high level of achievement, and indeed it is, but I am laying it out as the ultimate goal –taking priority over other goals that we have been taught to value, such as financial, social status and others.

As humans, we can increase this energy by drawing more of it in to our bodies and also by using it in our lives. This energy is also known as charisma. Why do some of us have access to this charisma or life force, while others do not? To begin with, our over-soul energy storehouse is increased by the positive use of our life force throughout our individual evolution. Some of the factors involved in building it include accepting responsibility for its proper application and use, while using it for the benefit of the advancement of humanity. While on Earth, the more we are tapped into the creative force, the greater our light, and the greater our power and responsibility.

Very often, some people who came into this life with

plenty of charisma did not understand their power and ended up misusing it. Because it is so tempting, if one is not careful, the misuse of power for egotistical means can result in self-destruction. While having more charisma has its benefits, it is also easier to spin out of control. We don't want to shy away from charisma simply because we have seen some people misuse it. Because we have not been educated on how to use our power, some people mistakenly believe it is easier to follow others, dim their light, or numb themselves with addictive substances. It takes work and constant refinement to build and balance this power.

In the new paradigm it will be increasingly important to arrive at new ways of looking at power.

Soul Searching…

Elvis Presley struggled with his, Michael Jackson couldn't contain his, Shirley McLain explored hers, Oprah has shared hers, and Betty White does a great job of aligning with hers while some people feel that they have lost theirs. One thing is certain: we all have a soul. It is the power that energizes us, animates us and directs us while we are in these human bodies on planet Earth, yet, we cannot adopt someone else's path or someone else's essence, we must learn to honor our own unique blueprint. If we don't like ourselves or wish we were someone else, chances are, we don't know what we are made of and who we were truly meant to be. Our bodies are designed specifically to house our individual soul blueprints and it is only misalignment that causes discomfort and distress.

Because each of us is at a different point of development, we will always encounter different choices as we go. Deep down inside, we may be the next Elvis or Oprah, but our placement on the spiral dictates that we become the best house painter or furniture salesman we can be first. It is good for us to know if we are hanging on to mundane things because we are afraid of the risks involved in reaching higher or if we are not ready to leap yet because there is more to learn. Knowing ourselves intimately and having a good intuitive counselor helps with this.

To know oneself is to know Heaven.

As important as it is to be in touch with our soul, we often find it to be elusive. How many of us know how our soul feels? Maybe you have met yours when you felt love or passion. Maybe you have met your soul in moments of silence. Perhaps you've met your soul when your back was against the wall and you suddenly pulled out a moment of genius or strength you never knew you had. I am pretty certain that you would not be reading this book if you had never experienced a time when you felt truly connected to your greater self. We need to remember the times when we felt aligned to Source energy because these memories help us to get re-centered when we are feeling off.

In order to demonstrate that we have distinct and palpable blueprints, people have conducted experiments where long time partners were blindfolded and challenged to identify their mate from a lineup. This is a very interesting concept and would probably make a great learning tool for workshops.

In our search for the inner light, we meditate, take yoga classes, read spiritual literature, attend church or consult oracles. We have heard gurus and religious zealots say that the true self is realized when all attachment to things of this world are relinquished. The main focus of teachings of the Kabbalah, which was kept hidden in earlier centuries, is focusing on becoming one with God. The truth is that there is value in all of these vehicles and we learn which ones work best for us as we go. We may make use of the wisdom of many spiritual philosophies and modalities as well as personally devised or borrowed affirmations to keep us in line.

All spiritual modalities should espouse going within.
Choose what works for you.

Even those who know full well how to quiet their monkey mind and listen to the still small voice have trouble getting there and staying there at times. Just like anything else on earth, there are some undeniable natural laws that come into play, and there are individual choices that may be used to enhance them.

We need to live with Love, clarity and soul alignment in order to experience Heaven on Earth. This state has nothing to do with our surroundings. Some of us may find ourselves surrounded by sheer horror and despair and have no other choice but to see whatever light we can. I have heard of prisoners of war telling stories of the inconceivable acts that they were witnessing. They said that the only way they were able to stay sane was to forgive their captors. Some of us have trouble forgiving even the slightest of human missteps. We can make these choices despite that which we find ourselves surrounded by as well as that which we have previously experienced and are still carrying around with us. Achieving a state of Heaven on Earth is also called ascension and almost everybody who is incarnated at this time is programmed to ascend!

Alignment with our soul gives us clear inner guidance, creativity, health, peace, joy and satisfaction.

We have created a society that is very enamored with the thrill of being entertained. Concerts, sporting events and movie theatres are big business and big draws for consumers because we need to be entertained. For many of us, ordinary life can be very lackluster, so we seek that which is outside of us – enjoying events that seem larger than life at times. Wouldn't it be nice to live like a child again, excited about each new day and all the adventure life brings? If this were the case, we would not have to seek so much of what is outside of us in order to feel alive.

One of the main reasons for fatigue is lack of alignment with Source energy. Our soul gives us energy for the things it wants us to do. When we block out our inner guidance, we essentially block out our life force energy.

Creative people of all kinds - painters, writers, performing artists know that they need to be in a certain place inside themselves in order to create or more definitively speaking, co-create with Source to produce something that others will enjoy or pay good money for. We love our entertainers and artists because they take us to a better place when we enjoy their work. In effect, they act as something of a placeholder for the cosmos and often have the power to bring us back to the fold.

Although we place artists and entertainers on a pedestal, we also have the ability to access the creative portal, which is the same as our instinctive center - our seat of wisdom. We all have different reasons to access the creative portal, whether it is as an entertainer or artist, or any other task in life. It is a matter of spending time there and seeing what develops on an individual level. Even if we don't have much time to explore this side of life, we can start by using what little time we have.

Even if we are not destined to be an artist or performer, it is possible to use this same portal to navigate the things of life, to communicate and to make good decisions. When we first begin to use intuition and instincts to guide us, we have to be careful to also learn discernment or we may jump to improper conclusions about the information or instructions we believe we are receiving. It is wise to take things slowly and learn to discern energy signatures and fields of consciousness, topics that are covered in subsequent chapters. Discerning these things is ultra important skill refinement involved in gaining useful guidance. Only that which comes from a higher source is truly valuable.

Remember as a youngster, being in school and wanting to play and explore? Our inner instincts were trying to direct us, yet we were told to ignore them and to pay attention to the books and the blackboard. We were taught by authoritative people at a very young age to ignore our instincts and that our worth was defined by our ability to submit to the authorities - the authorities outside of us, not the authority that dwelled within us. This is the primary reason we have produced a world full of sheep who believe all the media hype instead of a world full of strong, empowered, self-starting, self-sufficient people. People lose sight of their inner power when they buy into the bad habits of the herd.

When it comes to education, we have been teaching children the same way since the industrial revolution when we needed to train little robots to work in factories. I'd like to see people rise up and fulfill their purpose in designing new education systems that will instill values and presence of mind in our brilliant indigo and crystal children.

Because we have been so trained away from the awareness of our soul and our inner guidance, it will take time and patience, both individually and as a group, to learn a new way of living. Rebirthing is a step-by-step process. I believe that where we go wrong in our thinking regarding the concepts of intuition and creativity is that we tend to believe that either you have it or you don't have it. This just is not so. With the right tools, anybody can become aligned and clear. This requires a state of allowing because we are designed to be intuitive and creative.

Most of the time, we just need to get out of our own way.

In the process of re-birthing, we begin by recapturing the enthusiasm, curiosity and joy of our youth. We need to nurture the child within and take this precious being with us wherever we go. We need to forgive those who imprinted on us because they did not know any better. They were busy dealing with their own issues and doing the best they could. Carrying around blame will only hurt us in the end anyway.

We have a tendency to lose our patience or believe that we are doing something wrong if we don't get it fast enough or if we have to keep getting back on the horse. We have to practice forgiving our selves and others, but we also need to improve our ability to take responsibility for our part and not hang on too long. With this set of psychological tools in tow, we strengthen our ability to evolve. Esther Hicks, who channels the teachings of Abraham says, "You will never get it done, and you will never get it wrong." This does not mean we make endless excuses for hovering in the sludge, but it puts life in a more workable perspective.

Letting go of judgment will create a clearer state of mind and improve perceptive ability as well as enhance spirit communication.

Because each human soul is on a course of evolution that is much like a spiral, it is difficult to know where one really is in their climb. One may have a nice home and a great job and be very materially focused, while another may have great creative abilities while struggling financially. These two people may be entirely equal in their evolution if the souls of both of the individuals are engaged in a path that will balance the physical and the creative. The materially successful one will encounter life events that open up their center, while the creative one's endeavors will eventually bear fruit, gaining recognition and financial rewards for their work.

In order to circumvent the drama involved in competition and power struggles, our primary focus needs to be on getting to know ourselves while trusting others to handle their own path. Unless we have access to very detailed, historical information in regard to a certain individual, we will most likely misjudge them. Additionally, those involved in families of varying sizes often encounter difficulty when the individuals choose to embark on a course of self-discovery. In order for us to move neatly into our next cycle as humans, we need to get accustomed to letting go of each other while gaining higher levels of security within ourselves.

In the level of consciousness known as the Akashic records, there is a history of all of the evolutionary data about each being. In the absence of Christ Consciousness, we will always see people from our own limited perspective, but the Angels and the Masters see things through the lens of pure unconditional Love and have ready access to the Akashic records. The teachings of Abraham's law of allowing has its roots in the understanding of the spiritual nature of individualized curricula and the power of releasing people to their own path of attainment-trusting the energy to land them safely back home – the same destination we all seek in our heart of hearts.

As a spiritual medium, many people come to me with a list of questions about other people. We need to get more focused on our own piece of the puzzle because it is the only one we are in control of. People will not leave us just because we have untangled ourselves and as a matter of fact, hanging more loosely will provide for more joyful relationships. If people are meant to be in our lives, they will be.

The extent to which we have lost touch with our inner self varies by individual as well. It really depends on the influence that parents, teachers and peers have had on our individual personality type. Becoming intimately familiar with how the people and experiences of our lives have imprinted our personality and our energy as well as how we have allowed these events to either create discordant energy or help us evolve, is a step by step, one day at a time proposition and it does not happen over night. When we break down and analyze the dynamics of our psychological and spiritual development, we re-map our past and redirect our destiny. Not all spiritual teachers agree with this, however. It is up to the individual to decide what works for them.

Some people are more affected and manipulated than others and outer influence affects each person in a different way. We all come into each incarnation with a set of highly personalized and complex issues to work through based on our life history, soul goals and astrological influences. For this reason, I believe it is good to get really familiar with our personality type and our triggers. With the goal of being on center as the ideal, we can work to see what is causing us to lose track of our place of wisdom and power as we go through our days - and why. Journaling helps to identify our vulnerabilities.

Sometimes the drama and chaos flies at us so quickly that it is difficult to sort it all out. We will have to forgive ourselves over and over. Once we get the past sorted out, then we have to make sure we reflect daily on issues that make us uncomfortable, and get things sorted out so that we don't get the system clogged up again.

"The intuitive mind is a sacred gift and the rational mind is a faithful servant. We have created a society that honors the servant and has forgotten the gift."

Albert Einstein

Getting back in touch with the instinctive self...

Modern life has caused us to become too physically focused for our own good. Much of what we have become is the result of herd mentality and cookie cutter identities. While we are good at being part of the herd, we have lost touch with our true identities. From a metaphysical viewpoint, we are ungrounded and disconnected. These factors are the cause of the malaise in the world today. If we can learn how to be true to our selves and align with our paths, we will live in peace and harmony with each other and the Earth. Inner harmony and alignment create the state of energetic integrity.

The energetic world or the unseen part of life functions under a different set of laws than those of the kinetic world and this is one of the main reasons we have difficulty integrating the two. This is not to say that while we are on a spiritual trek, we should avoid or disregard physical laws. It simply means that we need to take a closer look at the undercurrents of life and how they relate to physical outcomes. The road to perfect integration begins with understanding that true power and clarity lies in the ability to allow the spiritual to drive the physical. The physical cannot drive the spiritual, so the spiritual will always win in the end. It is much easier to follow our spirit to begin with.

At times, the fear of the unseen or the unknown prevents us from making healthy changes. There is so much beauty and magic in the world and within each of our hearts. In order to look deeper into our soul, we must be comfortable with feeling deeper. For instance, if we are aloof when we really want to express Love, we clog up our feeling mechanisms. Continuing to withhold or mask our real feelings creates blockages and eventually causes illnesses. Avoiding our depth also reduces our capacity for joy and our ability to use our instinctive center for intuition. In effect, we distance ourselves from our true being when we avoid our feelings. This pertains to all feelings – whether they are loss, Love, laughter or anger. If we handle them properly, they do not have jagged edges nor do they wax and wane. Our juices are flowing like a beautiful, life-giving river at all times and under all circumstances. There is great power in this knowledge.

While we should not stay in a state of pain, sadness or anger long enough to brood over it, we need to go there if we are feeling it and deal with the issues related to the pain. We should rise out of the state with a refreshed feeling of exuberance and a new viewpoint, if we have dealt with the lessons involved in the highest manner. These things teach us about our self, our imprinting and our history. As we become clearer in our feeling center, we become stronger in our instincts, creativity and guidance.

If we allow our feelings to take us into the depths of our being, they will walk us right into a greater place of wisdom and then propel us on to the next level of existence – only if we allow them to. Very often, when we go deep, we begin to cry. So often we are tempted to stop ourselves because it feels too raw and we have a tendency to feel silly. We have not been taught that the act of crying and expressing tears takes us to a better place and we need to embrace this and see it as strength now, instead of seeing it as a weakness.

When we initially go inside, we will find everything that we have put there throughout our lifetime. This can be a bit of a Pandora's box. We may find things we didn't even know we stuffed down. The thing is, if we stuff things and don't process them in the highest spiritual fashion, we will be acting out in ways that we may not be too proud of and encountering turmoil in our relationships, becoming jaded. Additionally, we will continue to attract the same old circumstances over and over as a result, we end up ingraining our experiences into our chemistry and adopting them as our identity. It is much better to re-write our story and chalk things up to lessons learned, effectively taking a step up the evolutionary ladder.

I once heard the story of a woman who quit drinking and ended up crying for an entire year, all the while re-leasing the hurt that she had accumulated over years of denial. There was just too much stuffed down for her to process everything, so the crying did the large part of the releasing for her. Nonetheless, she did need to go through the process in order to heal. Crying is actually a very good practice as long as we don't go into self-pity. It is a valuable tool for releasing pent up feelings. Through this process, we also re-sort and re-file events of our lives. Ultimately, crying is the opening of the soul and is not always related to sadness.

Crying is one of the most common manifestations of going deep into the heart chakra.

Fully embracing and expressing our feelings does not mean taking others down in the process, blaming or be-coming destructive to our selves or others. It means that we need to get comfortable with going deep and finding out what is really in there or what is blocking the good feeling stuff. This is something that should be done be-tween our selves and God or a very good counselor or friend. After clearing out the feeling center, we need to allow time for integration. After a period of integration, we begin to notice changes in our lives.

If we have allowed ourselves to feel love, express our selves, cry and dream; we will have imbued ourselves with a much greater capacity for creativity on all levels because these acts of human nature create a well that is deep and wide. The feeling center needs to be clear in addition to being large. If we are carrying around pain and blame, then we have allowed our experiences to rob us of our clarity and peace, and we have diminished power to create.

One of the reasons that highly creative and unusual people sometimes come across as a bit crazy is that it has not been the norm to learn to practice the art of bringing to Earth the unmanifested, while keeping all planes of existence into a balanced state. As a result, we find it difficult to be connected and also function in the world of form. This lack of development is an attribute of the larger group mentality, while there are those who have figured out how to be the eccentric while walking among the flock. It can be tricky and I invite more of those who have creative urges and a desire to blossom from a soul level to come out and play. Let's get better at accepting each other's individuality and eccentricity. If we do so, it would be of great help to all of humanity.

*In the Golden Age, more people will
embrace their inner gifts
and we will have more stars and less super stars.*

The good news is that we can heal any thing that we find in there with the right spiritual tools. I must say, this is one of the things that I love about the new age-we have brought about new ways of restoring purity to our lives and learning to live again in very positive ways.

Our feelings are the gateway to our soul. Our soul fills up our body by sending our life force throughout our energy centers. Our body is intended to be an out-picturing of our soul, and the energy centers represent different parts of expression and thought. We develop these energy centers throughout our lives by the input we allow and the thoughts and feelings we express. This is one of the reasons that people have such unique appearances, even identical twins. This concept is the fabric of some healing modalities that recognize the symbolism and interconnectedness of the parts of the human body.

*Obtaining true alignment with our soul energy
brings a certain level of health as a result.*

That said, a person who avoids their feelings, stuffing

them down or internalizing them in a negative fashion often develops heart or digestive problems because these behaviors affect the heart chakra, solar plexus chakra and related energy pathways. All discordant energy creates energy blockages in the region of the body where the carnal mind is out of synch with the soul. Because the soul has God-like characteristics, it cannot fit into a vessel that is riddled with discordant energy. When we are loaded up with blockages, we lose the connection to our instincts and intuition and ultimately our health as well.

> *Each individual comes into life with*
> *a unique set of challenges and goals.*

If we accept the things that come into our lives as learning tools that are specially designed to advance and enhance our personal evolutionary curriculum, we will then process things in a more spiritually healthy manner. Events that we judge as seemingly difficult or insurmountable are likely to be our best teachers and our greatest gifts. In the book, Bringer's of the Dawn, author Barbara Marciniak makes one of the most brilliant references to this concept that I have ever heard: "It is like the Universe is dumping gold on the lawn and we are complaining that it is ruining the grass."

We have to learn how to follow and honor the energy

that is moving us through our lives if we want things to improve. Because our soul is in charge, it will provide us with more energy for the goals it has laid out. Sometimes fatigue is attributable to the fact that we have shut our self off from Source by ignoring our soul. When we ignore our soul, we close ourselves off to our supply of universal energy.

By now it should be clear that while the cookie-cutter life used to be the ultimate goal or the American dream, in the future, insofar as spiritual goals are designed, it is not. A generic blueprint does not teach us anything of value. The ultimate goal is to fulfill one's unique destiny.

Connecting to our soul is a learned discipline.

Because it is easy to get distracted, we need to commit to a spiritual practice of any kind that works for us, and discipline ourselves to stick to it. It is up to us to make the decision. For the most part, spirit is not going to drop down in front of us and hit us over the head to try to get our attention, although it sometimes does so and it usually is not pleasant when it happens this way.

I have heard many stories of people who were so distracted by a frantic life and endless list of things to do that they found themselves getting caught up in the rushing around, bickering, frustration and anger that ensues

– only to be awakened by a tragic error that would not have occurred if they had been focused and centered. This is also what causes people to forget their children in cars while they dash off to the office. I know of at least two people who suffered permanent damage and or inadvertently killed loved ones because they let a fit of rage get the best of them. These events are horrible, but indicative of the lifestyles many of us have adopted. We do not have to learn through tragedy or near death experiences. We will learn and it is pretty much up to us how we will learn. How will you choose?

Developing our awareness of spirit and receiving the strength and the gifts that the energetic world brings to us requires time, dedication, discipline and patience. It is a building process, much like learning in a class or building muscles. Staying connected to spirit may or may not be automatic, depending on the individual. It also requires a great deal of letting go and open-mindedness because it will present us with entirely new experiences and thoughts as we go.

Having our consciousness nestled deep within our bodies, grounded and centered in spiritual light, is the place that Esther Hicks is talking about when she is referring to the Vortex, but this can only occur and become an easy space to maintain when we become familiar and comfortable with it. This means we need to seek it, embrace it and spend time with it in order to get comfortably familiar.

The instinctive center or feeling center is the communication vortex between our soul and our bodies and is like a vessel that we either neglect or make good use of. It could also be viewed as a spiritual muscle. The more we use it, the larger and stronger it becomes. When people begin a spiritual journey, they are often instructed to learn how to be still and go within. This can be confusing to those who are not accustomed to focusing their attention on their inner being because we are trained to be outwardly focused, easily responding to this stimuli from years of exposure and repetition.

We can learn to respond instinctively once again, through practice and dedication, while unlearning the practice of internalizing the outside world. Spirituality is the process of learning to come from the inside – out. When we learn to respond to our instincts, we begin to take right action (or refrain from action) in regard to life's events instead of creating more karma. This may also be referred to as tapping into the un-manifested.

Tuning into our clear inner guidance is key to walking and following our unique path.
Everybody knows his or her self to a certain extent. I have met some people who tell me that they have no talent or

creative ability whatsoever. Some people, on the other hand, were blessed enough to have parents who spotted their talents and put them in special schools from a very young age. I always encourage people to do the things they love even if they are not going to develop them as a profession. The things we love to dabble in are very important for staying aligned with our spirit presence.

In addition to enjoying activities that sing to our heart, there are the little things we love. We need to develop healthy habits around creating sacred space. Sacred space may include anything from the jewelry we wear to making our house a relaxing haven. Most really wealthy and successful people are very good at tending to their bodies and their space −nurturing habits that serve to keep our lights shining in the cacophony of the world that surrounds us and often threatens to consume us. When it comes to attracting our desired circumstances, we must begin by demonstrating to the Universe that which we want. Starting small is better than not starting at all.

We must also have our quiet and our still time and learn to enjoy having nothing to think about and nothing to do. I have heard people say that they have tried meditating and nothing comes to them. This is because we have to learn how to be still and focus on our center for a long period of time before it is ready to begin processing information for us. To begin to receive inner guidance without the discipline of stillness is the same as a beginner driving a car too quickly – the driver would easily loose control. At times our soul puts us in a void simply because our body or mind needs rest. We need to embrace this concept in order to become efficient, effective and energetic. I am one of those who have had to really get disciplined at appreciating down time and silence.

This too becomes a learning process as we learn to understand the language interaction between our earthly self and our spirit self. Also, if there is pain, blockage or clutter there, it must be healed by talking it out either internally or externally and going through a forgiveness process or by crying and releasing. Stored up blockages can keep us from enjoying the stillness of the moment. There are many books regarding the process of healing and many practitioners of different modalities versed in this art, but there are some general and easy to use practices that should help clear blocked energy. Intentional breathing, prayer, yoga, energy clearing exercises, expressing, journaling and color therapy are readily available at any given time to most individuals.

Sweeping in front of our own door is how we heal the world - one soul at a time.

The stress of the world is simply the clashing of egos.

Imagine how life would flow and thrive if everybody was acting and functioning from a place of spiritual integrity and purity. Heaven is ours for the asking and the nice thing about this is that we don't have to wait for others to do it. We can achieve a state of flow and synchronicity even if others don't seem to be on the same page as us.

Laws of metaphysics dictate that all things must conform to the highest vibration available. Therefore, because being soul centered carries a high vibratory frequency, it will cause others to raise their vibration as well. This is something we all must know. We do not exist in a void.

I would like to emphasize that if we rely on certain people to help bring us back to center, we may want to wean ourselves of this habit because the people we rely on for strength will inevitably become unavailable and this is too great a responsibility to put on somebody else anyway. People relying on another to make them happy or bring them back to their moorings is one of the most destructive forces a relationship can endure, and unfortunately this has been the norm in the old paradigm. When people cling to each other, the issues of co-dependency rear their ugly head and life becomes a battle. True power lies in knowing that we carry this strength with us at all times and it is spiritually healthier to allow ourselves and others to evolve freely.

If we each dedicate our days to beginning and ending in our hearts and focusing on the growth of our soul and allow others to do the same, we will be doing the greatest service that we can do for humanity and the benefits will be tremendous.

Putting it into practice:

Spend a day focused on the breath…

There are many ways to get in touch with our inner self, but the most important one is to pay attention to the breath or the center of our being. Because our breath is our soul as it initially manifests into physical form, it is one aspect of metaphysics that the soul seeker cannot live without. Even if we have completely lost ourselves, we may begin again by calming our mind and listening to our breath going in and out of our body. This is a guaranteed start over point and we don't need help from someone else to get there.

When we gently draw in a breath we refocus our consciousness and realign with the wisdom of our soul, often gleaning insight for a given situation, refreshing our cells and our brain with Source energy, ultimately separating us from the chaos and cacophony. The trick is to stay in this place long enough to begin to feel the connection. We may also use gentle breathing to clear discordant energy out of our aura and our holographic field. If we stay in this space for a few moments, the answers will start to come into focus.

Upon gently breathing, we should feel at least a certain level of peace, clarity and strength. If not, that means that something in our chakra system is blocking this good feeling. We have to regularly practice looking inward and discovering the issues that may be blocking us. Journaling, watching for repeated patterns and doing general clearing exercises are things to do in order to gain improvements in energy.

Centering/Grounding/Clearing Exercise:

Any time you don't feel centered and feel that you have given in to the chaos of your mind and others, it is time to stop and get re-centered. Not only is it a good idea to do this in times of stress, if you do it a few times a day, things may not even get to the point of chaos.

This exercise is an integral and life giving ritual. You will need to learn to still or calm your mind by letting go of thinking and calculating. You will also need to learn how to become aware of where your consciousness is because you will need to bring your consciousness into your feeling center. Neutrality is also necessary because this exercise involves bringing Source energy in to your being to clear out old patterning. Judgment will jam up the process.

Each component of this exercise involves a unique discipline, so you may be good at certain aspects of it while others may need work. You may not know what you need to work on until you try to do the entire ritual.

This ritual is an important thing to do before pulling cards or asking spirit for an answer:

Begin by finding a quiet place to sit down. You may sit in any position that is comfortable, but I suggest that you don't twist your body too much. The main reason for this is that you need to be focusing on your instinctive center for this to work.

1. Clear thought processes and judgments. The mind and the brain should feel light – as though the wind is blowing through it. Empty, empty, empty.

2. Take a few cleansing breaths and release stress. If you feel any amount of stress leaving your awareness, you are doing a great job.

3. When you feel that the mind is clear, bring your consciousness to your center and try to feel your breath filling up your entire center, from your hips to your throat.

Envision and draw the breath into every aspect of your being and feel yourself attached to the floor and to earth.

4. Stay in this place and continue gentle breathing until you feel a desired level of peace. You will feel renewed energy because you are oxygenating your cells and bringing your soul into your body.

5. Picture tremendous amounts of light and love around you, holding you, guiding you.

6. Realize that this is your natural state of being.

7. If there is resistance anywhere, search for the cause. Is it coming from your own restrictions or judgments or is it coming from interference?

8. Once you feel this connection, either stay there and get connected to inner guidance, clear energies or simply continue with your day.

Make a list of things that bring present moment joy and awareness and continue cultivating the practice…

One other way we get in touch with the inner self is to become familiar with and honor the activities that have a great tendency to bring us back into the fold and feed our souls. For some of us it is spending time in the sand and swimming in the ocean, for others it may be comedy, taking a leisurely drive, and still others find solace while engaging in a physical activity such as gardening or exercising. Love of self requires a knowledge of that which refuels us and energizes us.

Spend as much time as possible noticing the difference between the head and the heart...

When we get into the vortex of Source energy, we need to note how we are feeling about things and learn to discern the difference between reality and ego. Is this coming from my heart or from my head? This is the type of work that only we can do to make our lives and our relationships better. The Love in our heart should be met with Love on the outside and we should feel its warm embrace. If this is not the case, we have gone into the void space in our minds or that of someone else's.

Any time we are not behaving or responding in a way that we are proud of, we can always take a time-out from life and listen to our soul. We need to give ourselves permission to check our alignment any number of times throughout the day and we must make this a personal choice and not wait for the permission of others to do so. It is a good thing to know when we need to re-center.

What thoughts and feelings take you into joy and which

things take you away from joy? Where are these things coming from and whose voice is it you are hearing?

Make a commitment to set aside a designated time for introspection…

At the very least, connect in the morning before the day is begun and once again at nighttime to reflect upon the day. I believe this is what many religions have intended when instructing their followers to pray or attend church. This is clearly the purpose of the Sabbath in orthodox Jewish religion.

Spend time acting like a child again…

Set aside a day here and there, or a block of time when you don't have to answer to anybody. Try approaching the day much like a child and don't plan anything. Practice present moment awareness and try to follow your instincts. You will hopefully begin to feel your youthful curiosity and enthusiasm creeping back in. Try very hard not to judge yourself. Notice everything around you and keep your breathing slow and steady. Feel your feet on the ground and notice the smells in the air. Do this as often as possible and you will begin to see how the life and energy becomes more alive both in your body and your circumstances.

These elements are the practical application of a spiritual term known as grounding. Grounding is a matter of really being in your body in the moment, completely connected to source. It is a sensational feeling when we do it right.

Make a change and carefully observe how it affects your interactions with others...

When we get really adept at staying on center during our idol time, we can take this practice out into the world and experience serendipity and synchronicity on an even greater scale. When we keep our brain cycles down and keep our crown chakra open, it allows the spiritual energy to disseminate from our centers and because it is a strong force, it draws others to their center subconsciously, unless they have very strong resistance.

Make lists of things you want...

When we write down all of the things we have always wanted to do or to and begin doing them, even if we only take baby steps, we send out a solid message to the Universe. We only have to start engaging in activities that we know are our unique talents and contributions, give them time to flourish and grow and then the Universe will follow suit. We have to create the energy impetus by actually beginning to walk in the direction we choose.

Demons, Dimensions & Deities

Matthew 4:6 "You are the Son of God", he said, "Throw yourself down." For it is written: "He will command his Angels concerning you, and they will lift you up in their hands, so that you will not strike your foot against a stone."

The human experience may seem difficult at times, so I believe it helps to understand that we really do have unseen guardians available to help us at all times. Some say the physical plane is the most difficult plane of existence. It is likely the most difficult because it requires a blending and balancing of many different levels.

I am the kind of person who has always felt I could tough it out and handle things myself. I remember the first time that I truly became aware of the need and the power of angelic protection when I was in a jam and said to myself, "I need ten thousand angels," and then immediately felt a shift in the energy that surrounded me. Our guardians are there at our beck and call, 24/7, but we don't always feel nor sense their presence unless we are tuned into their frequency.

We may also think of our higher self or over soul as one of our guardians. It just depends on how we view ourselves. If we view ourselves as helpless meager beings – that will be our reality. If we recognize that we have a powerful cache of energy at our disposal from our higher self and our guardians – that will be our reality. As a matter of fact, our higher self is our main guardian and it remains in contact with all of the other deities throughout our lives, whether or not we access it.

The more we work with Angels, the more they make themselves available to help us.

How is it possible to be in communication with Archangels? Do they take appointments and zoom around in the ethers going from place to place? How can one person be talking to Jesus in New Jersey, while another person is talking to him in the Philippines? Why do we experience random apparitions and occurrences of otherworldly contact – one moment it is there and the next moment it is gone? Why does someone flash into our consciousness and then cross our path shortly thereafter? Is it possible that everything we do affects every other person on the planet? Are we really protected by Angels? The answers to these and other questions lie in understanding the nature of our vibrational Universe and the different dimensions.

The connections that we have are indicative of the fact that we live in an infinitely complex multiverse connected to the same creative Source with intertwined realities or quantum entanglement.

A Course in Miracles makes reference to the various dimensions when it uses the phrase, *level confusion*. If we understand the concept that we and our brethren only make errors in judgment, or karmic missteps, when we are in the state of level confusion, then we find that it easier to forgive people who behave badly. We only behave in ways that are not angelic when we lose our track of our spirit self and become connected or entrenched in unsavory elements. We all have our good days and our bad days.

Upon acceptance of the fact that we live in a vibrational Universe with everything connected through quantum entanglement, it is easy to see that we all contribute to the energy of each level and therefore we are connected and responsible to and for each other as well. While there is overlap and mingling of the levels, that which is created from the place of the soul or unified field should be the leading feature of this plane of existence. Think of it as putting your best foot forward. What we are witnessing in the world today is the result of thousands of years of mis-creations.

A master is able to manage the frequencies and func-

tion very well, while carrying out their divine plan.

The teachings of Abraham refer to the Vortex, which is the place of divine co-creation. Also referred to in the teachings of Abraham as the un-manifested, this is a place where all is well – at least as far as spirit is concerned. Because the dimensions are shades of all different frequencies and very often enmeshed, if we don't pay attention, we can get caught up in the rip tides and underlying currents of all kinds of energies. First, we need to learn about their characteristics and their behavior and use alignment and intention to stay properly focused. Then, we have to practice grabbing onto them and staying in their focus.

It requires a high vibration and focused discipline to keep the realms balanced and in harmony.

While we learned about math, history and physical science in school, the field of metaphysics teaches us about the physical properties of the spiritual world and it is indeed a very intricate science. We can learn from others, but we benefit most by taking the time to study our own soul and psyche – becoming ever more familiar with our personal idiosyncrasies and habits.

Part of the reason that we go in and out of contact with the divine is that we don't know how to get there and once there, we don't necessarily know how to stay there and many times we are not aware of the thoughts, behaviors and actions that cause us to eventually lose track of the connection. It is up to us to notice the subtle triggers that cause us to lose focus and it takes vigilance and practice.

Multi-dimensional communication and consciousness are much more complicated than we can imagine, so I am going to lay down a simple foundation of understanding so that anybody can begin to tap into this valuable resource.

As humans, we only have to have a certain level of understanding in order to work with other dimensions. We must be careful not to overthink things of the mystical realms. Until we have evolved to a certain point, where we comprehend and receive information in large blocks instead of simple sentences, we need to put a great deal of trust in the divine.

Those who have had occurrences that were clearly of the Angelic variety know that they have very little ability to clearly explain the experience in earthly terms. It is very difficult to put spiritual experiences and metaphysical laws into human language, but we do our best. On the other hand, attempting to navigate life without using spirit connection and communication is difficult, stressful and tiring. As long as we have this power available to us, we may as well use it.

As I mentioned, it is important to understand that because we are living in a place that is denser and of a lower vibration than the spirit world, it is necessary to simplify things and narrow them down in order for our minds to make sense of them and apply them to our reality. If we spend too much effort trying to figure it out, we end up defeating ourselves in large part because we are over-engaging our logical mind, which cannot fully comprehend the etheric planes anyway. This ability to trust our spirit connections is called faith. We must put these concepts into practice in our daily lives in order to develop them. As we integrate spiritual practices, the higher vibrations will show themselves to us.

In reality all of life can seem magical with practice and intention, but we need to stay grounded.

In order to even begin to comprehend the other planes of consciousness, one must first discard mental and philosophical ideas based on our hard reality because the spirit world does not look or operate the same way as the physical plane. We look out on a world of separation, brought about by the mechanical nature of the physical plane, yet when it comes to mysticism, we are asked not to take that which we perceive through our physical senses too seriously.

In any event, the physical plane is actually not as solid a reality as one may be led to believe, although our senses say it is so. Also, it can be interpreted in countless different ways as egos have a strong tendency to judge things from a very narrow perspective.

One of the advantages of working with the higher planes is that there is more consistency and agreement there than on the physical level because we are tapping into the unified field or the unmanifested.

It is through tapping into the un-manifested that we usher positive change in the physical. The great heroes and scientists throughout history were tapping into the etheric realms and that is why they impacted humans the way they did. They were able to access information and discoveries that would benefit the masses and in the end they fulfilled their destiny by becoming vehicles for change at pivotal times in the evolution of humankind. Some people such as Oprah Winfrey and J. K. Rowland, knew that they were fulfilling their destinies through their careers. They demonstrate what is possible through steady alignment with the higher self and purpose.

The more of the un-manifested that we can bring in to the physical reality, the more we will experience Heaven individually and collectively. I believe that connection to the other side is something that can be learned and is beneficial to all humans. It is similar to many scientific modalities in that it can be broken down into components of study and it can be mastered.

As far as I am concerned, faith has a scientific foundation – one that we are really just beginning to study. I don't corner the market on this thinking because there are religions that take a more scientific approach to spirituality such as Christian Science, and Science of the Mind and Church of Religious Science. These churches have been around for a long time. It is just that we are now taking this type of thinking out of the fringe and bringing it into mainstream society more than ever before.

Science appears to be meeting us in the middle. As accepted norms in science change through the years, building blocks of creation of ever diminishing size are being discovered. Scientists have been confused by the fact that each of these realms has its own set of rules, some of which they become privy to and some of which they are mystified by. The smallest particles, called quarks, are able to bi-locate and re-locate in an instant - qualities that denser particles do not possess.

In 1935, three scientists, including Einstein wrote a paper on a subject they referred to as quantum entanglement. The paper suggests that objects that have been broken apart at one point in time, maintain a connection that causes them to simultaneously carry out given behaviors even though they are seemingly no longer in relative proximity to each other. This theory is correct and it is a clue as to why we can contact benevolent beings anywhere at anytime.

These scientific discoveries should be enough for us to begin to trust in the other world and understand that two worlds with different rules and properties can co-exist and co-operate. Instead of viewing these major categories as separate, as we evolve, we will blend the two for the best of both worlds.

Science has already demonstrated how matter has morphed and re-distributed as the Universe has unfolded and evolved, carrying with it, traces of origin. On a smaller scale, our electricity exists on a grid and therefore, we are interdependent and connected on that level. A power outage in one location creates outages hundreds of miles away depending on the connections involved. Buddhism emphasizes the ripple in the pond effect that each one of us has with regard to all of creation. Everything we think, feel and do goes into the field of the whole even though we feel we are drowning in a sea of humanity.

We will only perceive and experience that which we are ready for.

I find it interesting that mystics and intuitives often find themselves having to explain or defend their beliefs. We should not feel so compelled to explain. We should just be happy we have made these connections and focus our energy and efforts on our progress.

Trying to convince others about the spiritual realm is usually a poor expenditure of time and energy. Furthermore, it is not really possible to explain things of another plane of existence to one who has not yet experienced it. People will experience what they will on their own schedule.

Why is it that we don't ask the non-believers to prove that the spiritual planes do not exist?

Many years ago, we could not have comprehended what has become available to us through satellite communications and cell phone signals. In many ways the fields of consciousness are similar, partly because the connection is made via pulses and electrical transmissions, similar to current technology.

Spirit communication and the quality and vibration of the different planes of consciousness actually have electrical signals, but they are too small to be detected by existing technology. At this time, only the organic and sensitive nature of the human energy system is able to master the discernment of the etheric planes. Mechanical equipment does not vibrate high enough to do so at this time.

In addition to humans, animals are also tapped into this stream. One day we may develop mechanical equipment that is sensitive enough to work with the subtle energies, but until then, we are it.

Recognizing the planes of consciousness...

Our sensitivity and ability to recall energy signatures is what we use to align with the subtleties of the different frequencies or matrices. Tuning in requires that we slow down, be mindful and use our feeling center. This is a learned ability that develops throughout lifetimes and must be practiced regularly in order to refine it. It needs to be used and tested over and over again which is something that we must do of our own volition. Here again, we have access to genius and recall that is impossible to explain.

In attempting to explain this subject, I am fully aware that those who have never touched on the other side or don't actively remember touching it, will not be convinced or intrigued by this topic in any way whatsoever. It is not really possible to explain the invisible. It is however possible to help refresh the memory of those who have been there and to help reinforce and empower them to continue to explore this realm.

Our soul holds the memory of so much more than we realize. It is already familiar with the connections to the higher planes, while the brain has trouble understanding the properties of the non-physical planes. The brain cannot comprehend the concept of nothingness and it cannot comprehend the concept of no-time, no-space either. These are not precepts of the physical reality and are not part of the plan or rulebook that it uses. When we are in a place of utter disbelief and feel cornered mentally, then we learn to know that this feeling can only occur when we are too focused in our logic center and in our heads. It does not matter how much reasoning we engage in sometimes – the brain cannot comprehend everything that our souls can.

As a matter of fact, when I was very young, while enduring one of my sleepless nights and clearly in a state of meditation, a voice said to me, "There is something less than nothing." What this did for me was clear the space in my mind for endless possibilities. We must create this space before our mind can accept things other than how our brains want to perceive reality. If we hold on to the little messages we receive out of the blue and store them in a place that we call curiosities, the ego shouldn't mind too much!

I mention the idea of nothingness because it creates an open template for the mind to begin to put things that it finds when connected to the un-manifested. The mind then has a choice as to whether or not to accept realities outside of that which it believes is acceptable or normal.

When the switch is flipped in the mind (the vertex be-tween the brain and the spirit), then the channel opens. This would explain why disbelievers often do not experi-ence the etheric planes. They have not flipped the switch and are essentially blocking the channels. And as we all know, blocking something does not negate its existence.

During those times when we get caught up in our heads or in our questioning mind, we must talk it down and calm it. It does not hurt to develop inner dialogs for this issue.

In addition to that which we have a level of control over, I have recently learned from a colleague of mine, Rich Ralston, that there are programming blocks in some people's minds that must be removed before the crown chakra can open to the endless possibilities of the spir-it. These programming blocks may come from any of a number of different sources. Whether or not this is the same as flipping the switch, I am not completely sure, but it is worth exploring. His book is called The Subtle Energies and is available on Amazon.

Naturally, we will also continue to gain greater under-standing of these studies as we evolve. A large part of the advancement in all fields, including science, will involve the mainstreaming and validation of the etheric energy fields. As we gain a better understanding of the energetic undercurrents that drive our existence, we will also be advancing the science of health and care of the human body during this shift, which is very much needed.

Certain energetic healing modalities such as acupuncture and chiropractic already recognize and work with the connection between energy points in the body and have gained recognition for their superior healing qualities. There is a host of other energy healing modalities as well. The best way to work with energy is to really open up the mind to all of these connections as well as the ones that exist in the Universe. Once we open up to the possibilities, things become more evident in time.

"The significant problems we face cannot be solved at the same level of thinking we were at when we created them"...Albert Einstein

The physical and astral planes beckon us through our five physical senses, and therefore have great deal to do with their propensity to distract us from our connection to the spiritual planes. They seem to be more readily available and easy to understand. If discernment and intention are not applied to our daily activities, the over abundance of data flying through the channels will distract us and pull us off center. We begin by making the connection to our vortex or our inner guidance a priority and make sure we are regularly aligning with it.

We don't want to drift off into the ethers and have an out

of body experience either. I have been at group prayer meetings of all kinds when some folks left their bodies and had to get help from the others to get back into their vessels. It does not serve a purpose.

When we find ourselves doing the proverbial head slap, it is time to shift our dimensional focus. So, we know that Heaven lives within us, but yet we often find our selves wandering the hinterlands, trying to find our way back. Each individual has their triggers, and there are common reasons that we all find ourselves going off track. We can go off track for a few moments, a few days or even years.

In order to stay tuned to the higher frequencies without getting ungrounded, it is imperative to balance the energies of the physical planes with the spiritual planes and have the ability to work with both simultaneously. We stay aware of our physical body and our physical surroundings, but we allow the spiritual to dominate our presence.

The spiritual plane is always there and broadcasting to us even when we are not tuned in, yet we need to have a desire to tune in and learn how to recognize its vibration or energy blueprint along with a commitment to align with it. This alignment is what is intended with modalities such as Yoga and Tai Chi. Both modalities involve intentional breathing and it is in the breath that we find a connection to spirit.

The spiritual connection provides us with a warm glow from the inside out. It provides us with a secure and joyful feeling and makes us feel fulfilled at all times, no matter what the external circumstances are. Any feelings other than those that are related to Love are a manifestation of another plane.

A spirit driven life requires the right balance between the mental and the spiritual.

"Man thinks he lives by virtue of the forces he can control, but in fact, he's governed by power from unrevealed sources, power over which he has no control."...David R. Hawkins, M.D., Ph.D.

The Mental Planes and Monkey Mind…

Actually, we connect with the thinking of untold others when we are in our heads. This is the origination of group mentality and caution is needed because and we can fool ourselves into believing that we are connected for a noble cause and get caught up in the excitement when in fact there is no other solid basis. Being in our head is not good for these reasons, but also because it will give us mental fatigue, give us wrong answers and give us headaches. The awareness of this issue is so critical that I suggest isolating this subject and working on it for some time before attempting to move into the other spheres. Once we tame the mind, we can explore the spirit.

What we conjure up in our carnal minds has nothing to do with the true reality and people seem to be astonished when I say this. It can only know the past and its own experiences. An accurate image of the larger picture and co-creative information do not come from the carnal mind. Unless we give the ego a back seat and learn to illuminate it with our instinctive center, we cannot believe anything it is interpreting or projecting. Just because a drama is playing out before us does not mean we need to take it seriously.

It is never too late to choose differently, douse the past in Heavenly energy and turn it around – or walk away and choose a different course. However, before we walk away, we make good on our contribution to the drama if it will help heal the situation.

The strongest distractors humans face are the mental and the astral planes.

When I make reference to the head, I am referring to the brain and to the carnal mind - that part of the mind that is materially focused. Because the carnal mind and the spiritual mind exist in the same energetic space, we need to be the decision makers and the captains of the ship. The mind is actually the vertex between the brain and spirit and that is why there is confusion as to whether the mind is a concrete occupational space in our brains or part of our spirit function.

As a vertex, the mind is the connecting point between the two distinct worlds and not distinctly a part of either. It is more like a computer flash drive that makes choices whether to give credence and attention to the brain or to the spirit! The human brain is much like a computer and is best for storing information that it has received in the past. It can either be the receptor for spirit or the reactor, depending on how we direct it. The soul has a strong influence over the choices of the mind, but the mind will waiver and lose focus if we are not attentive.

The human brain is wired for action and desire, which is purposeful, but it can get too ambitious and overwhelm itself by attempting to process too much and going off into tangents. The mind is also wired to be receptive to our spirit, which is positive and calm through all events. The trick is to achieve the necessary balance in order to carry out the motives and desires of the spirit.

The necessity to choose between the lower and higher self is not unique to spirituality and Christianity. This dilemma is aptly captured in the Hebrew concept of Yetzer Ra. Yetzer Ra is the disposition of the human mind, having been entitled with a free will. The will of the individual may choose between Yetzer HaRa - alignment with the animal self, or with Yetzer HaTov - the eternal spirit self. If we don't train our minds to be more receptive to spirit than the things that beckon us on the outside, we will continuously experience insatiable desire for external satisfaction – which is where addictive behaviors and a host of others come from. Although a human is complex, there is a distinction between the lower and the higher self and the choice is ours.

It is in our best interest to choose to respond to desire from within and to develop correct action rather than to give in to the animal side, which overtly focuses on survival, planning and calculating. Our spirit side knows how to balance and harmonize our existence as well as to guide it. Our spirit is also intuitive, while our carnal mind is not.

Whatever direction we choose, physical or spiritual, will continually increase, so we must be careful how we choose at all times.

Altered states obtained by the use of Peyote, LSD or methamphetamine or even inhalants have been mistaken for spiritual experiences. People believe they are attaining an altered state, when in fact they are just creating a different state, which does not have anything to do with spiritually higher states of consciousness. Dulling our senses or crossing our wires does not make us evolved either. These are some of the errors of the past.

A spiritual high releases the same feel good chemicals with no side effects and it is derived from a shift in perception.

Rather than trying to dull or twist the mind into something unsustainable, training the mind to focus inward to the instinctive center instead of in the carnal mind is how we stay balanced on the fence and is extremely difficult for adults who spend a large part of their time and energy focused on daily tasks and stresses. I have been practicing this for years and still find my self up there in my head, but I know how to catch myself when I begin to feel head pressure, lose present moment awareness and begin to toil mentally.

Recognizing the characteristics and behavior of the different states of awareness are keys to ascension and mastership.

The Astral Planes…

The astral planes are considered to be somewhat of a debris field of discordant, low vibrating energies that are non-physical. Often when we are open, but not clearly spiritually focused, we become subject to this field, not only because we sense its presence and feel that we need to examine it, but it seeks us out as well. Examples of astral plane energies are trapped spirits and accumulated thought energy that has taken on a life of its own.

Amateur mediums, low vibrating hosts or unsuspecting sensitives have all been duped by this field at times, the likes of which have given credence to the fear attributed to the unseen realms throughout history. These fear induced perceptions are likely the reason that the Bible and many religions warn of false prophets and so on. At any rate, we can choose whether or not we want to learn about the astral planes. However, one must recognize its energy and behavior to avoid deception. This subject bears at least a certain level of discussion because it is likely that it will be encountered when on a quest for communication from the other side and it is also a field of endeavor that brave souls who study it offer up as a service to others at times.

I once helped a young woman who believed that her spirit guides were trying to get her to fast and drink only water. In addition to convincing her to believe this ill-derived information, they were shaming her. I was able to tune in to the frequencies that surrounded here and informed her that these were opportunistic trickster energies that benefited by latching on to unsuspecting individuals who are vibrating at low enough frequencies for them to latch on.

By fasting and going into fear, she was subject to going out of body by becoming ungrounded and that is exactly what these spirits want. When we go out of body or become severely ungrounded, we are asking for trouble. When we hear voices that seem to be whispering in our ears or locked in our heads, this is usually from astral energies looking for a place to play. Our spirit voice resonates inside of our instinctive center and uses our own sensory equipment to decode, decipher and relay information for us. Our inner voice should sound like our own voice and so on.

These trickster energies grab on to people who have given in to fear and other low vibrating behaviors. Very often, drug addicts and alcoholics become hosts to these energies because the frequently drop their vibration to extremely unhealthy levels. The physical body becomes disabled by the ingested substance, while the spirit drifts out of the body in to sometimes dangerous territory. This is what happens when a drinker has a black out period. In this way, addicts and alcoholics often become somebody we do not recognize and they also behave in ways that they would not otherwise.

Any time we fill our minds with hateful thoughts, abuse our bodies and engage in unhealthy thinking in general, we take the chance that we will drop our vibration so low that we become hosts to the astral plane. This is why some humans have committed evil deeds that are incomprehensible to us. Evil acts by humans are the result of their giving in to the dark forces and allowing their will to be taken over.

What has occurred on this planet time and time again is that the group mentality ends up manifesting itself through one ungrounded individual or group of individuals. Everything we think, do and feel ends up joining with the same issues in the ethers until it reaches its breaking point and must manifest as a physical reality. This is why we all bear responsibility for the actions of humanity because it is simply a matter of the age-old saying, "If you are not part of the solution, you are part of the problem." We don't change the world by telling others what to do; we change the world by shifting our energy and behavior.

Humans are not evil, but they can become hosts to dark energy

I believe that disruptive or intrusive spirits come through via varying circumstances and that they show themselves in different ways and to different degrees. As humans existing in a web of many dimensions, we need to be careful about crossing the lines and becoming a host to these scavengers.

Although the subject of trapped energies is controversial, I have to say that I have personally experienced a great deal of communication with energies in the astral fields and have been with other people who were sharing the experience, so I am convinced of the substantial nature and importance of this science. When people need help interpreting ghost activity for instance, they seek the help of a medium who is able to clearly interpret the desires and activities of the trapped spirit. Because of my spiritual education and experience, I am able to communicate with these types of spirits without being pulled into the astral planes. Delicate handling is required.

Something I really enjoy doing is exploring hauntings. I recently did a walk through with the manager of the haunted Iao Theatre on Maui. This theatre has received press coverage through the years and the ghost sightings and tales have endured for decades. As is usually the case, the spirits come out in force when I arrive on the scene because they are looking for an opening and they recognize my energy. In addition to the spirits that were hanging around the building there was large pockets of old energy from past activities.

In many cases the dense clusters of energy were imprints left behind through the many decades that this theatre was in existence. Built in the 1920's, it had gone through many phases and much of that had been imprinted on the various rooms and hallways. A well-trained and experienced medium knows the difference between a spirit presence and an energy imprint, while all types of heavy energies are often interpreted by the layperson as a spirit presence.

It is important to understand this concept because opening ourselves up to guidance opens us up to many, many things, including the astral planes. Also, we will be completely confused by the thinking of those individuals that we have an energy connection with, but we will also have added confusion because we will pick up the processing of our neighbors, etc., mistaking the urges and information for inner guidance. This is just another reason to consider taking things slowly and behaving like a student.

The Spiritual Planes...

The connections on the etheric level are best viewed as webs of information. These realms don't exist in neat little packages and lines like the things of the physical dimension. It may help to see the etheric realms as smoke, drifting and twisting, stretching, expanding and contracting - undulating currents that are far reaching and that permeate everything.

Most energy systems are a conglomeration of energy, yet all must contain higher energy or the energy of creation in them somewhere. By tapping into Source energy, we bring more of it into all energy systems we encounter.

Any Source energy we weave into a system stays there infinitely.

The spiritual planes are the place where benevolent energies such as Christ Consciousness, Archangels and high vibrating spirit guides reside. Christ Jesus achieved an ascended state on Earth, therefore giving us a physical reference for the portal to the spiritual realms. It is my belief that he instructed his followers to remember him as a way to come to God. He embodied the Spirit of Creation itself, but is not God. Christ knew that he was connected to Source, and since the people of the era where having trouble tuning into God, using him as a focus would help bring clarity. After all, God is in everything. It is time for us to recognize this.

Christ Jesus wanted people to understand that they would find the salvation they were seeking by focusing on him, rather than seeking connection with God through the faulty and archaic practices and idol worship that they had previously applied. This works the same way as any other spiritual practice that helps the seeker remember Source energy/God. This does not mean that focusing on Christ is the only way to find Source. It is not the only way, but it is a good way. Christ Jesus is only one of the Ascended Masters that we may call upon.

As a matter of fact, The Christ vibration or the members of the Legions of Archangel Michael have populated the planet at certain times in history. The appearance of the Christ vibration on the planet during the lifetime of Jesus was pivotal in our evolution and served the purpose of seeding us for the millennia to come. This same soul family is incarnated here at this time to help the planet move into the fifth dimension.

I don't believe that Christ Jesus ever meant to have people believe that he saved us or took away our sins. I believe that his true words and true motives have gotten lost in the translation and are often misconstrued. I further believe he demonstrated to us that we have to take responsibility for our behavior and have a spiritual focus every moment of our lives.

The soul family of the Christ vibration has reestablished the course of the planet by becoming the embodiment of Source energy and has recently reestablished the grid foundation for the unfolding of the spiritual blueprint of the planet. For more on this subject, my book, 144,000 Points of Light is very helpful.

At least a portion of our soul is eternally connected to this Source because it is where from we were created. We could view this connection as an umbilical cord if that helps. Since we always have this connection, it is a matter of nurturing it and practicing it. This is place where all things are creatively and harmoniously connected. We cannot go wrong when we align with our spiritual vortex. Only egos clash because they have their own agendas. Source will never lead us astray.

When connected to Source energy, we feel uplifted and the grip of the physical not as strong. Things go smoothly when we are connected to the highest vibration or in the vortex. Groups of people, when connected and functioning primarily on the soul level, experience an earthly manifestation known as synergy. It is as though everybody has become one when they are tuned in together. Most dictionaries describe synergy as: the interaction or cooperation of two or more organizations, substances, or other agents to produce a combined effect greater than the individual contributions. Great things have been achieved through synergy and co-creation. We will see more harmony and synergy in the new paradigm.

We get along best when connected in the unified field of consciousness wherefrom creativity and genius flow.

Prime examples of they synergistic phenomenon would be The Beatles and other song writing duets such as Simon & Garfunkel. It is interesting to note that as soon as the parties began to squabble over who was the more valuable party in the creative endeavors, the flow of creative energy puttered out. Not surprisingly, the synergistic groupings, once disbanded, were never as successful as the group was together. I am not sure that the participants recognized that there was synergy at work in their earlier success. As soon as they brought ego into the mix, the vortex collapsed. This is a very powerful place and we have the ability to enjoy synergy with the creative force itself when we let go of ego.

In the fifth dimension, we will work together

more harmoniously because of our alignment.

The spiritual realm has an energy signature that bears all the facets of Love. The behavioral aspects of Love are trust, honesty, tolerance, gentleness, joy, defenseless-ness, generosity, patience, faithfulness, and open-mind-edness, thankfulness and expansiveness. On a clairsen-tient level, it is soft, energetically vibrant or significant and it has depth. On a vibratory level, it has power and dominion over other levels or vibrations. Once this fre-quency is introduced to an energy system, that system will eventually come into harmony or alignment with the creative force. Love is basically the trump card of the deck. This is a metaphysical law.

When we seek and embrace this realm, we bring it into the world and make it available for others to log on to. This is how we affect untold others when we make the choice for Heaven. Everything we touch will eventually turn to gold! When we allow our ego self to get out of the way and become conduits for God's will, landscapes magically transform.

It takes a tremendous dose of selflessness to relinquish all goals of the ego to claim this space, but the results are that spirit takes over and spirit guides us and ultimately speaks to us through our inner being. Life becomes effortless as we allow for expansion. This is evidence of the power of surrender.

If you want to change the world, increase your capacity for Love.

Spirit guides us through our instincts and it can also guide us through wise advice disseminated through the ethers from benevolent sources. When having a desire to communicate with guides or Angels, it is imperative that we are tuned into the right station. The clearer we are in this field, the more likely we are to actually hear verbal guidance or feel the Love of our Angels that surround us. Even when we are not completely tuned in, we can ask a question and wait for an answer, which may manifest in any number of ways.

Answers may come as a knowing or an epiphany. Someone may come up to us and raise a conversation or make a comment; we may see a message somewhere and realize it is meant for us. Some of us will hear a voice and some of us will be shown in other ways. We can use forms of divination, but must be careful with these. People with varying vibrations created forms of divination such as oracle cards and we also need to get our selves in a good place before we can work with them. If we are in a bad place, we will pick cards that reflect our stinking thinking, rendering the experience useless or allowing trickster energies to come in to play. This is one of the reasons that so many Christians have turned away from their use, but it does not negate their overall value.

Choose oracles that were created with a high vibration.

Doreen Virtue, Ph.D. has many books published by Hay House Publishing, and has created a wealth of oracle card decks that serve the purpose of helping people work with the Archangels. Because I believe that Virtue is the world's foremost expert on all things angelic, I highly recommend selecting some of her work for fun and learning. This is probably the best way to get familiar with the tone or frequency of the Angelic realms because she has clearly fulfilled her purpose by bringing this work into the world.

When we work with the Angels, our burden is lightened and we actually are able to feel the difference, both mentally and physically. Very often, we will feel magical tingles (not the heavy ones associated with astral energies) or even see sparkles in the air. We may see colors floating around or smell flowers in the air. I know someone who had a globe of light lead her in the dark when she was a small child. I have had things change right before my eyes. Signs of angelic assistance take many forms.

The Angels communicate with us in ways that we can understand and they are always there as long as we want to work with them. They have unconditional Love for us and know us intimately. I think that sometimes people don't want to acknowledge the ethereal help that we have been given because they feel ashamed that another being, even though their Love is unconditional, may know our personal business. If this is the case, it is imperative to get past it if we want to work with angels. This type of thinking can be reversed just like anything else.

I can feel heavenly Love around me most of the time. It joins with the Love I feel in my heart and I can sense its warm undulations holding me and giving me a sense of security in a turbulent world. If we tap into it, it also helps soothe nerves and stiff muscles. The Ascended Masters and angels in the spiritual realms are our spiritual teammates and we need to invite them in and learn how to tune into their guidance by aligning with their frequency. We will not feel their presence if we are filled with fear and hatred.

Bridging the etheric and the physical plane…

All of creation does not express itself solely as groupings of visible objects much like the manifestations of the physical plane, and separation is the result of the limited perception of our carnal mind. There is a great deal of matter, both seen and unseen in the Universe or Multiverse, with the larger part of creation existing as that which is unseen and highly malleable in comparison to physical matter. On all levels, creation is held together through the law of attraction, which is a multi-disciplinary science in and of it self.

We each need to develop our own idea of what the unseen looks like as we build our perception. The way we picture the unseen may also be indicative of how we are relating to it as well. Our impressions of creation or God need attending to if our impressions are not uplifting. We can go back in our history to find the imprinting and clean it up. Lack of experience with or distortions of the God force are not reasons to turn away. I have heard that people's perception of God is a reflection of the imprinting of the parents. God is a brilliant, loving force that is forever uplifting. Perception can be healed. If one does not like to refer to creation as God, then so be it.

Although the interdependence and connectivity of creation is complicated, we can isolate various energy systems and learn how to work with their qualities. In the new age, we have been recognizing the different modalities and developing and polishing them in order to create useful applications and to refine the science thereof. When developing our personal guidance and connection to Source energy, we also need to isolate those practices that we need to polish, study them, work with them and then blend them with other things to obtain eventual mastership.

Spiritual work is similar to the rigors that an athlete goes through to master their sport. Athletes work on their swing, their stance, their musculature, their stamina, mental focus and so on. When all disciplines are working well and working together the athlete performs at levels that the average human can only dream of, but it takes practice and repetition.

So when it comes to mastering Heaven on Earth, one has to master the realms that are available and useful to the carrying out of spiritual destiny on planet Earth before they can be truly effective.

The events of our lives serve the purpose of refining our mastering of the different planes and this is why we need to understand that we will never obtain the highest vibration if we push away our challenges. Many spiritual teachers understand that everything that comes into our lives is specifically designed to take us back to our soul – not to take us away from it.

When we can hear our Angels or guides speaking, recognize signs and feel the Love – they will guide us

Additional pointers…

*While it may be interesting to learn about the astral

planes, string theory, out of body travel, past life regression, for the purposes of navigating our best life now, focusing on our own creative force is the first foundation we need to build. When we are stronger we may learn about other things.

*Creation is NEVER in fear or hatred and alignment with it always brings peace. Get to know the difference between being in alignment and out of alignment. Ask yourself often, "What channel am I tuned into?" Make it a habit to stop activities and interactions when feeling out of sorts and re-align your frequency and raise your vibration. This is a great way to take responsibility for your contribution.

*Flow and synchronicity only happen when we remain in the higher planes and follow our instincts instead of logic. We can't use both man-made tools and spiritual tools to navigate. They are like oil and water. Doing so will cause confusion. Spirit is very smooth and magical. Synchronicity and manifestations defy explanation.

*Allow your definition of a perfect planet to evolve as you journey on. You may be surprised by what you find with an open mind that is free of preconceived agendas.

The following exercises will help to identify these energies and how they work in our lives.

Ask for spirit communication...

Ask your guides or ask the Universe to reveal something to you. For instance, if you want to know what your greatest contribution to society is at this time in your life, you may ask the question and then slow your mental postulations and be patient while the Universe delivers your answer. This usually produces results within 24 – 48 hours and it may come to you in various different ways. Not only is this a useful guidance tool, it also helps you to begin to understand how your inner communication system works. This will also help you to see that you are wired into a connected delivery system.

Try to feel the energy signatures...

Whenever possible, feel and learn to discern different energies. In order to do this effectively, practice being neutral toward energies and don't let judgment cloud your spiritual vision.

Recommended Reading:

Daily Guidance from your Angels, by Doreen Virtue, Ph.D. and other related publications.

All Oracle Cards from Doreen Virtue, Ph.D.

The Power of Now, A Guide to Spiritual Enlightenment,

By Eckhart Tolle

Subtle Energy and the World We Experience, by Rich Ralston

Creating & Maintaining the Light Body

The spiritual new age has brought about a wealth of information to enhance our ability to heal all levels of our being. We have created new modalities and have resurrected and refurbished some ancient practices – all of which address the holistic and integrated nature of our being and our Universe.

Naturally, in order to experience bliss, our bodies, which are part of our personal energy system, need to be as healthy as possible. In order to be healthy, we need to consume healthy and natural nutrients to the extent possible and we need to incorporate high vibrating thought processes as well in order to maintain energy integrity. Understanding how perfectly balanced energy should function and flow through our bodies is a developing science, just like anything else. I am sure we will continue to learn, especially as we give the field the credence and attention it deserves.

Source Energy flowing throughout our personal energy system allows our body to achieve homeostasis

While we must be conscious of taking care of our body, in the areas such as diet, rest and exercise, energetic integrity is vital as well to providing a healthy flow of life-force energy through the physical body, allowing it to seek homeostasis, which is the state of wellness and proper function. Yes, through the inherent natural feature of homeostasis, the human body is programmed to seek wellness. The only thing that stands in the way of this feature is earth and ego energies, which permeate our being on all levels, either enhancing or prohibiting proper energy distribution. When we make discordant choices, our energy flows get interrupted and then our body pays the price. It stands to reason then, that managing our egos and keeping our vibration high are the best ways to enhance our body's natural ability to heal and one of the main things we actually have control over.

One could study volumes of text explaining the ways in which we clog up our energy as well as the remedies we may apply to heal the energy blockages, but nothing speaks louder than experience. I recommend choosing one bit of discordant energy such as worrying about money, which is very common in humans. Then, spend one hour or maybe two, not worrying about money and observe what happens to the body. Any ego attribute will work. Almost any length of time will work as well. This little experiment works with all uncomfortable or discordant energy.

There is an immediate shift in physical well being

when discordant energy is removed

Once having experienced the magic of choosing a higher vibrating thought, I hope that many will become encouraged to do the work necessary to achieve optimal energetic health. I say work because it requires us to make a change and stick to it instead of taking a pill. Some energetic changes are easy and quick while others will take more time and require a bit more digging. Often it takes weeks or years to change old engrained habits. Milestones include one week, three weeks, one month and then one year. If something has not been cleaned up and cleared out by the one year mark, something was not done right.

We carry our history in our bodies and our chakras. A key feature in healing discordant energy that is stored in the body and the chakras is to rewrite the story in a positive manner.

We create karma in part because we make errors in judgment. Much of what we have experienced was meant for our own good or for the good of all humanity, but we often take it personally and integrate it into our story as a hurt or a negative. If we begin to view everything as something that we can use to propel us upward, no matter what it is, we will be much better off. We can also go into the past and re-file historic information as well.

Everything created has energy, including feelings and thoughts. We can't try to escape this reality or tuck things away in a hidden place where it won't cause problems. Warehousing our past only blocks the way for new thoughts and avenues to flourish.

We are always creating because Source is always expanding. When beginning to work with energy, a basic understanding of the aura and chakras will suffice. Those who want to go into energetic healing modalities for a living or endeavor will want to take a more detailed approach.

Our busy lifestyles have a tendency to keep us from being fully aware of the minute details of our soul's intended growth.

Each of the energy centers or chakras that run through the center of our being are the vertexes between our soul and our physical self. They store and process areas of consciousness as they relate to existence in physical form. They are much like a computer in that they store information regarding our personal evolution and chosen experiences. For instance, the heart chakra or Anahata as it is referred to in Sanskrit, bears the lessons of Love that we have engaged our selves in throughout our lifetime. The extent to which we have embraced or disregarded these lessons will be out-pictured in our general heart health and related functions. We also have many minor chakras throughout the body. The most outstanding of these are on the hands and feet.

Each chakra represents a different area of development and either enhances or destroys energy in the regions of the body that it relates to.

When it comes to energy and physical health, the growth of the spirit is more important to the body than physical caretaking alone. I know of two wonderful people who were avid runners with impeccable diets, who astonished their friends and family when they had a heart attack at a fairly early age. Knowing how energy works, I was not surprised to hear the news because I had been aware that both of these people were rigid thinkers and were wound pretty tight. Each had always been very focused on strict physical regimens, while neither greatly displayed the ability to relax or to express themselves in creative ways. Both of these individuals were charming and polite on the surface, but deep inside the warmth was lacking. The softer aspects of life, such as warmth, creativity and laughter are the type of energies that keep healthy source energy flowing through our heart chakra in particular.

Furthermore, with regard to the heart chakra, neglecting one's inner voice or stuffing down feelings will also cause heart issues because the chest region is not getting the nourishing heart chakra energy needed to maintain homeostasis.

Good energy can override a certain amount of poor physical maintenance, but even impeccable physical maintenance cannot override poor energy integration.

Once again, the study of mind-body medicine in relation to the chakras takes a look at the very subtle energies of the body's energy vertices. It is a very extensive modality and there are books about it.

Mind-Body Medicine...

What we do in mind-body medicine is determine the mental-emotional aspects related to the energy centers that feed the different areas of the body. We may either sort through and work on the thoughts we have that create mental turmoil, or we may take a different approach and ask the diseased or uncomfortable areas of our body to tell us what is wrong. We can learn to listen to our body by stilling our mind or we may use the many references that exist to help us with this. We may also consult a medical intuitive. Drs. Mona Lisa Schulz, Deepak Chopra and Carolyn Myss have done much to advance the field of medical intuition and mind/body medicine.

Let's look at some situations where a person has discordant energy and then walk through the process of how a healing may be conducted:

Example 1: We have an individual who has constant digestive issues and tightening in the gut. This person encounters power struggles on a regular basis and often experiences blow-ups after periods of oppressing their feelings and emotions. Upon taking an intuitive look at the origin of the problem, it is clear that this person has trouble with power issues stemming back to their childhood. It is recognized that the parents misused their power and displayed obnoxious behavior as a result. Because the child does not have a good example of proper use of power, he or she grows up believing that people in power positions are obnoxious and continuously gravitates to individuals who confirm this version of reality. Conversely, a person who houses their power properly should be charismatic and attractive.

Initially, the fear of misusing power caused this individual to shrink back their power any time they engaged in a power struggle instead of learning how to develop it and use it properly. This occurred particularly when he or she was around others who had either real or perceived power over them. The energetic manifestation was a shrinking down of the third chakra – the ego's way of trying not to threaten someone else's sense of power.

This person also developed a deep-seated fear of setting someone off.

The initial impact of the improper posturing caused tightness in the belly and the resultant digestive issues and volatility became the out-picturing of the energetic imbalance. The oppressed feelings in this person ended up being counter balanced by a subsequent explosion of energy as the discomfort of the subdued energy center finally makes a circuitous maneuver, sending a signal to the entire inner communication system, creating an emotional explosion, much like a dam breaking. All of this happens primarily on a subconscious level and it happens so quickly and instinctively that the individual does not know how and why it is happening. Consequently, this person ends up engaging in the power struggle that they were trying to avoid, but ends up doing it in a way that is not productive because it is being routed improperly.

In order to solve this problem, the individual needs to first recognize that they shrink down around others with power. This may be discovered through introspection or meditation, help from an intuitive or by studying the meanings of the chakras. This person may want to view and study examples of people who properly use their power.

Approaching the issue slowly and intentionally, the subject will want to learn how to pick up on the subtle clues in their mental state or physiology that will let them know that they are about to retract their solar plexus energy. Then, they need to learn to keep that area alive and well in all circumstances by breathing into it, validating it, valuing it and becoming comfortable with it. By moving more slowly through the circumstance next time it arises, they will find themselves reacting differently if they allow the refreshed communication of the healed energy center to direct the interaction.

Until this discordant energy is healed, it will most likely end up being counterbalanced or mirror balanced by attracting a life experience in which this person has to deal with another who tends to misuse their power by attempting to overpower or diminish others. If the two individuals involved were holistically minded, they would both recognize their error and fix the problem by each standing in their power and respecting each other. Both parties embracing a healthy respect for their power creates an optimal situation where there are two power centers available for problem solving and manifestation, rather than having one dominate or block the other.

Here is where the hidden blessing comes in: This soul, having a goal of learning to use power properly in this lifetime, chose parents with power issues so that an imbalance would occur, causing the individual to have to work through various issues regarding power. This is also a great example of the beauty of law of attraction. These unbalanced, impure relationships serve the purpose of helping us work out the issues as long as we heed their presentation in our lives and go deep enough to find the root of the problem.

Example 2: I had a client whose life purpose was singing and speaking. Her life purpose had a heavy focus on the throat chakra, therefore rendering this area more sensitive to energies than another would. With a strong goal of expression, this individual should be singing beautiful songs and speaking inspirationally, but instead, and much in error, this person was very harsh and angry a large part of the time, speaking curt words to people at every turn. This type of personality would cause throat issues regardless of one's life path, but in her case this misstep created an even larger impact on her system.

Initially she told me that she and her husband had spent well over one million dollars on treatments and related expenses over a decade. She had gone to numerous specialists, downed countless pharmaceuticals, travelled the globe and then finally decided to try some energy medicine. The mind-body connection called for a restoration of the emotional center and the throat chakra.

Years back, her piano accompanist died suddenly, leaving her bitter, never wanting to sing again. There was a severe energy block in her throat chakra. This created negative energy in the emotional center as well. Because singing and speaking were part of the individual chemistry, shutting the throat chakra down and filling it with bitterness and regret becomes a double hit to the energy.

By the time she was 50, she had developed throat cancer and eventually held fluid in the lungs and around the heart. She engaged me twice a week to do energy work and healing on her body. She said that the Reiki removed all of her pain from the chemotherapy. I also counseled her about the other issues and she did find some relief when she let herself go and had a crying spell. As a result of the toxicity released through crying, she reported that she experienced relief in her breathing, but expressed that because the crying made her feel helpless and silly, she would not be doing more of it.

My client experienced a glimpse of what could be and I sensed improved energetic alignment. It was clear that she could get through this if she would do her clearing work, but did not want to do it. She took dozens of different pharmaceutical drugs every day from a doctor who had no knowledge of energy healing. She was resisting her energy work and her prescription drug intake was rendering her body's natural healing ability useless. Although she desperately clung to life, she died of congestive heart failure in the end.

My client's husband expressed to me that her passing did not sadden him, as he had been waiting for her to die for many years. This may have contributed to the counter-energy that held her in a state where she was subconsciously reluctant to do her healing work. The dishonesty in this coupling was very unhealthy and therefore not a healing channel, although she leaned on him quite a bit for financial and emotional support.

Karma ends only when a feeling is transformed into unconditional Love.

This situation brought to light many things for me as a healer. This was a clear example of the perfect storm of low vibrating energies that would do nothing to augment the millions of dollars the couple spent on her treatment. When a person is in such a delicate situation, so many things need to be working in harmony for a person to get better. The ill person needs a support system of high vibrating caretakers, the client needs to be willing to do their work and they need to have a doctor who supports holistic healing. No matter how badly a healer wants their client to get better, it will not make a difference if the other aspects are not in place.

Energy Enmeshment and Cords...

Our energy connection to others is a subject that is very

neglected. Without a working knowledge of this field, it can prove impossible to improve our energy and circumstances.

If we are energetically connected to another person, we may experience phantom or empathy pains. If connections endure for a long enough period of time, we may actually manifest another person's mental or physical disposition in our own body. I have witnessed first hand, many occasions where one member of a long-term marriage actually developed a serious illness from their spouse's discordant behavior or thinking. The one that stands out the most in my mind is the instance where a wife had developed symptoms of MS as a result of her husband's nagging and nervousness.

We need to take responsibility for how we treat others and carefully guard the energy we are generating at all times.

As humans, we have developed some bad habits with regard to energy enmeshments and they are all based on conscious or subconscious, karmic agendas. For instance, in the case of the wife taking on the husband's disease, there must have been an agreement somewhere in subconscious minds of the two, that the husband's personality is the wife's fault or responsibility. Taking on each other's illnesses is a part of the co-dependent nature of relationships in the old energy. We did a lot of this in the past, but in the new paradigm it is not wise because we need to use our inner guidance much more, and the energy of others will create interference.

Subconscious programming, soul contracts and agreements are not recognized in psychiatric studies. Using detailed information about the soul history is a necessary ingredient in the process of learning how to create more harmonious pairings and relationships of all types. This is a field that needs to be expanded in the new energy, but will be developed over time as those who were destined to become intuitive practitioners step up to the plate and do their studies.

We must also get more accustomed to allowing others to flow freely in their own energy and recognize that they must make their own choices and decisions regardless of the approach they appear to be taking. Even when we are in intimate relationships, we may not know enough of the details of our partner's history to call the shots for them accurately. It is good to loosen the reigns and trust that the people we are relating to will grow at their own pace and in their own way. As we evolve, we recognize that we get our best energy by connecting with Source, rather than taking it from another person.

Co-dependency creates more karma and should be avoided. These are the pitfalls of the type of relationship A Course in Miracles refers to as special relationships.

Most relationships do not serve us well because of mis-handled agendas and conflicts, in many cases preventing us from having a clear connection to our soul. We need to stop expecting relationships to provide us with that which we need to receive from Source.

Only relationships that function well on all levels will make it through to the Fifth Dimension

Most energy enmeshments are created by misplaced responsibility, clinging or blaming. Things are most often not as they appear on the outside because, especially in couplings, there are many interdependent hidden agendas.

Here is an example of hidden or buried agenda cording:

A boyfriend is corded into the girlfriend's heart chakra – The boyfriend needs her love and approval to feel alive. This connection makes him feel energized. She is ac-customed to being a caregiver and feels validated when someone needs her, so she agrees with the agenda on some level and lets him attach to her energy.

What happens as a result is that she begins to feel that she needs him because she is picking up the lack in his emotional body as a result of the energy connection and perceives it as her own through the energy of the cord. Two people are in effect living off of one energy supply. In essence, a once full and vibrant individual now suffers a lack as a result of the energy drain. This feeling increases over time and eventually she forgets how she felt before the relationship began and gradually loses her own identity. However, the fact that this occurred is an indicator that the affected areas are weaknesses and vulnerabilities that need attention. I call this mirror balancing.

Only the participants and perhaps a keenly tuned intuitive counselor who is able to access the Akashic records may know the intricacies of energy entanglements between people in karmic couplings.

The issues that tie us to another so tightly are highly personal and subconscious and often have their root in past lives or our experiences with our parents.

The couple's energy has now become a blur or distortion, making the discordant energy elusive, ultimately creating a situation where it is difficult to disconnect. The two have blended their realities and the line between the individuals becomes a blur. Long-term couplings can result in similar appearance and even similar handwriting. The different aspects of the individuals begin to fight for independence as their neediness sets off a tug of war. When the two try to separate, they feel emptiness and pain, all the while continuing to be drawn to each other. The only thing that would fix this relationship and the subsequent relationships of either of the two parties would be to find the hidden reasons behind the need to compensate through another person. Searching the past is a good idea in this case.

It is easier to clear a cord early on and it becomes more difficult with time. When we disconnect and or heal cords in order to improve our energy, the other person feels it and very often is not ready for the change. We need to talk to the other party either in person or soul to soul. We need to look at the subconscious or karmic agendas and then start the work necessary to change the behavior. If it turns out that the healing has to be one sided, then so be it. It can take a little longer to keep the cords from reoccurring if only one party has the desire to change the discordant pattern. In this case, if the other is resisting, we just have to repeat the procedure until the habits are changed.

It often happens that only one party involved in a struggle will finally do the right thing. It is ok if only one person does the work. Sometimes, one person's work forces the other to do their work. However, if we try to stick around and or expect the other to change, and it is not occurring, that person is not ready to change and we need to release ourselves and move onward and upward. That would be great if it worked perfectly every time, and though it is not impossible, we have to get comfortable with cutting people loose and continuing on our journey if all of our best efforts have not helped.

If we did the clearing right, we won't attract the same circumstances again.

In all cases it is best to seal the deal with love and blessings of peace. We have to realize that for the most part, we attract relationships into our lives for the purpose of clearing karma, learning about our true nature and making choices. We can hardly blame others for playing out the drama for us. There is always counterbalancing karma on our side that allowed the cords.

Ideally, people connect in the heart for closeness, communication, and energy giving and receiving. When we part ways to conduct other business in our lives, we should let go of each other's energy. We then trust in the perfection of the flow to bring us back together instead of eliciting promises or making demands. Less healthy connections are made for the purpose of one individual being possessive of the other and also in order to siphon off of someone else's energy. Cords are only appropriate for brief periods of time in healthy, loving relationships where there is give and take and also in the parent child relationship when the children are young.

It is good to be able to have enough faith in a relationship that we can connect when we are together and then flow back together at other intervals without hanging on to each other's energy. This allows all parties in couplings or groups to flow in their own stream instead of being smothered and stifled by each other. It takes trust in spirit to have a healthier relationship and this is what is meant by the phrase, "If you love something let it go; if it comes back it is yours, if it doesn't, it never was."

In a higher vibrating lifestyle, we allow our loved ones to flow freely, to explore and to make decisions so that they can evolve at their own pace and in their own way. When we allow our loved ones the opportunity to discover and follow their inner guidance, then we Love them truly. I have had to let go of many soul mates so that they could complete their journeys. It is a great gift and one that is very necessary to bless others with at this time.

We are not with others for the purpose of hanging on to each other and completing each other, we are meant to be in peaceful, productive partnerships and groupings.

Special relationships are the relationships of the ego or the wounded self. By working on the issues that created the cords, we then can experience holy relationships – those types of relationships that are based on a common purpose and serve the evolution of both the individuals as well as the planet.

However, we must always keep in mind that as long as we are powerfully drawn to relationships, we must heed their call because it is important to do our work. Until we become completely harmonized in our own being, we don't want to turn away from relationships simply because we find them difficult. The way counterbalancing or clearing karma works as we move through life is that we will always get an energy to mirror what is out of balance in us. For the most part, our relationships serve the purpose of showing us what we need to fix within ourselves. When we become more balanced and true to our soul identity, we will attract other more balanced people and then be able to get on with a more productive, peaceful existence instead of constantly having to resolve karmic issues.

If we don't attract others for intimate relationships at that point, then so be it. It is ok to be whole and traveling a solo journey. This time of karmic wrap up and flux is naturally creating many solo travelers.

Polarizing is another mirroring issue we get stuck on. I have seen pairings where the karmic reason for their meeting was to learn from each other. Instead of learning something from the other, each participant denies his or her issue, pointing the finger at the other. In time the two become so polarized, the situation gets blown out of proportion and appears silly to the observer, while it seems to make perfectly good sense to the participants. Often, people decide to go their own way in order to get relief from the tension, only to find the same relationship issue popping up over and over.

The polarizing phenomenon is very common with parenting issues. One parent is lenient and the other is stern and although both need to come more to the middle, the one who is lenient becomes increasingly more lenient while the other becomes more rigid. By overcompensating for what they perceive to be the wrong behavior in their partner, they become an exaggerated version of their self instead of making changes within themselves. I believe that many children serve the purpose of teaching their parents how to be good parents. It is interesting how the interpersonal dynamics work so well to this end.

This phenomenon is the reason we see so many couplings with opposite or compensating traits. We see type A's with type B's and so on – because they have something to teach each other.

Mirror balancing is a way of getting our attention and showing us what we are really putting out there as a beacon. Very often, we are only in touch with that which we would like to believe about our self and the mirror balancing shows us our shadow self, or the one that is hidden from us. If we are enablers, we will find needy people who drain us. If we are in fear of danger, we will attract thieves and criminals and so on.

So, when things happen in our lives that we do not like, whether they are catastrophic events or relationship strains, we need to step outside of our self or consult our intuition to determine what the cause of the issue is. We dig deep to locate it and then do what we need to do to fix it so that it does not keep holding up our flow.

The longer we have been involved in a relationship or a circumstance, the more we are going to address all the levels of our being in order to clear the energy and imprinting.

As long as we are reflecting on the past, we will keep re-creating it.

If we have a strong center and are familiar with our own energy signature, we can simply breathe and meditate any accumulated energies out of our field. We can expose ourselves to sunshine, salt water or other purifiers in order to get clear whenever we feel heavy and confused.

In the case of beginners or people who have a long history of abuse, substance abuse or any other type of stress of mismanagement of energy, it can be complex and an energy practitioner may need to be enlisted. No matter what the case may be, it is good to reflect, figure out what we needed to learn from the experience, thank it for the wisdom it brought us and then move on to bigger and better things.

Wise soul searchers use challenges as stepping stones.

If an individual does not have access to a healing practitioner, the prayer method can be used. We do this by asking God/spirit to guide us to the next step in our healing each morning when we wake up and upon going to sleep at night as well. The wisdom of spirit will take care of the unraveling, but it will be up to us to face the issues head on and heal them with Love. We may have to stop and research the issue by perusing books or the Internet.

We need to give our healing to spirit for a few different reasons. For one thing, it is wiser than us. Also, when we dwell on things to long, we make them too real – we give them staying power. It is natural for things to repeat for a period of time once we have left a person or situation, so we let go of them by applying energies of transmutation. We can use our breath to breathe them out and we can take each one as it crosses our path again and bless it and send it on its way, asking the Universe to bring us new, more appropriate experiences and people to advance us on our path. We can picture the people and events surrounded by white or violet light. I used to have strained interactions with large dogs, but by enveloping myself and any dog that I encounter with violet light, the tensions no longer arise; in time, they have dissipated completely. The invocation of colors works very well.

We have to continually run the filters and do the clearing until patterns and players; the old habits and the old circumstances begin to change. Some may have instant results and yet others may take years to achieve an energy shift. In the process, we also learn to neutralize our thoughts and often obtain a healthier, more balanced way of looking at the issue from the past as time goes on, as long as we apply forgiveness techniques and new ways of handling things.

Another thing we can do is to learn to step out of a situation and refrain from internalizing it long enough to get a clear and unbiased picture of it. When we depersonalize the dynamics of a situation, we remove the volatility and reactiveness, which muddies things. This is the reason we sometimes need to consult an impartial intuitive reading, but once again – we don't always have access to this luxury for various reasons.

We need to get comfortable with searching ourselves. We should be able to ask our self, how does this really make me feel and why? We need to let the feelings that we find inside talk to us without us judging them in order for us to hear them clearly. When we go into a deeply honest place inside, we often find fleeting feelings or thoughts that fly past the radar so quickly that we don't recognize them until they are trapped and put under the microscope. At this point, we examine where the feeling, behavior or thought patterns come from and work on changing them or replacing them with a higher vibrating, better feeling behavior and thoughts.

These things that hang around and keep repeating themselves are our triggers. They are the things that create volatility in our relationships and cause the arguments. They cause us to misjudge people and events. When we bring our wounded self to the table, we hold up progress and hurt or damage other people in the process. The purifying and clearing of our past is what A Course in Miracles calls Atonement. When we come to the point where we can sense our own divinity, we then can see it in others. Then, and only then are we able to do so.

Some folks believe that it is not necessary to dissect things and that there are things that don't need to be examined. I believe it is part of our evolutionary process to eventually understand this entire concept better and to be able to discern what to do in order to bring things into alignment with the highest energies. The discernment and treatment method with regard to mind body healing modalities is similar to the process a medical physician may go through in order to determine the order of treatment under their modality. They decide whether to prescribe medication, recommend dietary changes, run tests or any other variety of options. It is the same with metaphysical healing. Each issue is very specific and multi-dimensional, requiring a different approach or treatment for the different maladies we suffer.

*Achieving the physical state of perfect alignment with
higher consciousness is called ascension.*

By now, I hope you are excited about journeying to the other side. It can be as easy as flipping a switch or changing your perception, or as difficult as going through a couple years of therapy. Choose your modalities, your disciplines and your mentors. In the second part of this book, we take things further up the evolutionary spiral.

I will close with this beautiful reading about Carolyn Myss' revealing of the beauty within:

"I spent the day in deep reflection about the intimacy of the Divine in my life, all of our lives. I had prayed for counsel, necessary personal counsel. In the prayer, I released my hands from the steering wheel of my life, requesting that the Divine take over. I could feel that I was being directed to do something, to see something clearly - but what was it?

Finally, I uttered the powerful prayer, "Take charge. I cannot see my way." Within hours, a seemingly small incident occurs. It escalates. By morning, a heart-shattering event is the result. The answer had arrived. My life is drastically changed - just like that. I retreat by habit, by spiritual gravity, into the silence of my interior castle. I am breathless. A part of my life had just evaporated. I had asked for clarity. I had asked heaven to take charge. Now I must gather the pieces of the consequences.

In my castle, I sense the fracturing of my heart - and then - just like that - heaven sends in the remedy. The love of beloved friends poured in. I let that love flood into my heart like a salve on an open wound. I feel myself fall even deeper into mystical silence. I am now just a witness to the two sides of my heart - one fractured, one absorbing love. I remember the myth of the two wolves in a dark, cold cave, one pacing with bitterness and one calmed by love.

The cave dweller must select one to represent the consequence of the injury life had just given him. Which one will carry the wound out of the cave - the wolf of bitterness or the wolf of love? In times past, I've chosen bitterness and watched that wolf leave the cave on my behalf. I wanted the wolf to attack the world, as it had wounded me. I would not be responsible for those attacks - who could control a wolf? But that wolf only bit me - again and again.

Now, wiser, I chose the wolf that carried love. I visualized a silk thread and mended my heart in the darkness of the cave. I dwelled in awe and gratitude that a prayer uttered in silence while standing in my kitchen was heard with speed. Whispers reach heaven...I stayed in the silence of my castle for a long time, healing the fractured side of my heart.

And then I felt my rich, creature nature rise up and take its place once again in the vast expanse of my interior castle. I felt its sparkle and life force ripple into every cell of my being, animating my being. I could feel my essential self once again - this is who I am in this lifetime. Know thyself and you will know the universe...Today I bow to the intimate presence of God in my life - in all our lives."

Carolyn Myss

Recommended Reading:

Vibrational Medicine for the 21st Century and related publications, by Richard Gerber, M.D.

Power vs. Force, The Hidden Determinants of Human Behavior, by David R. Hawkins, M.D., Ph.D.

The Energy Healing Experiments, Science Reveals Our Natural Ability to Heal, By Gary E. Schwartz, Ph.D. with William L. Simon

The Intuitive Advisor, A Psychic Doctor Teaches You How to Solve Your Most Pressing Health Problems, by Mona Lisa Schulz, M.D., Ph.D.

Mind Over Medicine, By Lissa Rankin, M.D.

The Science of Ascension

I have discussed the new energy and introduced some of the benefits that may be expected when a higher level of consciousness takes hold. This section will help you to understand this and how to work with energy to restore your highest self and open up your consciousness. There is a formula and there is a roadmap. The formula, road map and blueprint is spiritual Love.

I will now be talking about integrating the facets of spiritual Love/Source energy/God into your being. You may have to revisit some of your past experiences and past relationships in order to re-create them by healing the energy, if they were not processed with the highest truth and purpose earlier on. If the result of re-processing is not a peaceful state of Love and acceptance – the karma is not healed. This process is called clearing.

When we clear, it is much like the process that computers use to de-fragment and clean up their contents. We gain clarity and energy for future opportunities when we clear out and re-file the past.

We experience Heaven on Earth when we live with Love, because in Heaven, only Love is real.

When we go through the process of clearing up old karma, we also allow our true selves to emerge and take hold on our newly ascended planet. It is wonderful to work with creation itself, but we have to be tuned into the correct station.

When we are aligned with Source energy, we can see the beauty that underlies everything. Colors are brighter and everything has greater meaning. We have access to answers and receive inner guidance more readily. Life also becomes much easier and enjoyable and we have more energy.

We may have some preconceived ideas of what ascension is and it most often is construed to be something very mysterious and for that matter – out of reach for the average person. All beings are connected to Source/God to some extent and that connection can be obtained and enhanced. It is a process and it can be very detailed and lengthy, but it is attainable for most people. All it takes is a commitment and a willingness to change and let go. Spirit will guide you every step of the way.

Most of us will have to re-write our story and put the past behind us.

Ascension may refer to the resurrection of Christ Jesus, or it may simply refer to the climbing of a set of stairs. The Internet is loaded with talk about ascension and it can be confusing. Some believe we have to leave our bodies in order to ascend. Some believe that otherworldly beings will come along and assist us in our ascension. Ascension is actually the resurrection of higher consciousness.

If someone tries to tell you that ascension is anything other than transforming your being or changing your perception, then they are being deceptive or they are seriously misinformed. There have been cults or mentally maligned leaders who convinced others that their salvation lied in giving up their belongings or even their physical bodies. None of this is true. There is no sacrifice involved – only blessings.

We initiate the process when we give our soul the go-ahead to restore our spiritual self. Actually, we begin our ascent by surrendering. Even if we surrender just a little bit, the energy will take over and take us back to our soul. It only takes a little willingness, according to *A Course in Miracles*, the mother of all ascension manuals. *A Course in Miracles* can be a lot to digest for most and this is why there are many books written about the course. I refer to it often.

Because there is so much information available on this subject, I am fulfilling the need to condense and simplify the mystery of ascension.

I recall my moment of surrender in this lifetime, and I surrendered it all – mind, body and soul. Because I completely opened up to the process, I went through a tremendous acceleration. I opened to the wisdom of my soul and information came flooding into my awareness at a very continuous, rapid pace.

I was not able to do much else for several months because I had such a tremendous backlog of unfinished business up to that point in my life. Up until my day of surrender, I had way too many unanswered questions as well. The backlog had to be taken care of before I could move on. Although I was relatively young, I was in the state of total dysfunction. My head hurt and was foggy; I was chronically fatigued and was not living with joy.

A period of time after my surrender, I had an aura picture taken. Although the actual picture shows indigo and violet, the print out from the computer referred to my aura as ultra-violet. Ultra violet light is measured in angstroms and it is in the x-ray spectrum. All colors have vibrations and our auras reflect our disposition. Embodying this color aura meant that I had effectively cleared out my old patterning and had fully integrated my light body. Most recently, I had another picture taken and it was pure white. In other words, I am qualified to teach this because I have attained it.

The lower human behaviors cause our auras to be any-where from black to red and the higher behaviors create auras that are in the color spectrum from green to white and beyond. I find it interesting that red and orange stars are not as hot as blue stars. This follows the same science as that of aura colors. The more Source energy that is integrated into a person, the hotter the aura. This healing energy is what makes a healer's hands get warm/hot. The middle of the palm has chakras that are connected to the heart chakra.

I believe that ascension is best understood and taught by those who have moved through the process themselves. Otherwise, the concept becomes speculation and open to great misinterpretation. We are in a time when an as-cended state is available on planet Earth because she is also in a high vibration. Our inner selves know this and most of us have come here to be a part of the new par-adigm. We don't have multiple lifetimes to achieve this state any more, so many spiritual teachers have surfaced in order to help others move through the process quickly.

Human ascension involves the integration of higher energies and the dissolution of lower energies.

We may exist in the state of ascension or we may be going through the process of ascension, which means we are on a positive upward spiral – feeling lighter and more connected every day. If we are in the state of ascension, this means that we have resolved all of our karma and have effectively transcended the heaviness of the physical plane, yet we are still here on Earth.

Our thoughts, attitudes and feelings create the energy or the vibratory field of our bodies. All of the ingredients that go into creating our composite vibration come from many places. While we do have many bodies – etheric and physical - for the most part, our bodies in the etheric are already aligned with Source energy, whereas our physical, mental and emotional bodies easily lose their alignment with Source because they are subject to so many earthly influences.

Keeping a high vibration requires regular maintenance in order to be a vehicle for our etheric energy. When the two are out of sync, we feel uncomfortable. When our physical self is aligned and harmoniously working with our etheric body, we feel free and light. Esther Hicks often speaks about being in the vortex. Being aligned with our true self or soul is how we get in the vortex. We may seek the help or advice of others, but ultimately, we own complete responsibility for our ascension process.

Our planet has held different frequencies at different times throughout its evolution and there have been times when higher vibrations were dominant and available. It is believed that there are some civilizations still in existence on our planet, yet they are not visible to lower vibrating beings. All of the vibrations have their own distinct realm, much like radio stations or IP addresses. In the case of dimensions and vibrations, there is a bit of overlap and blending, just like the progression of the colors of the rainbow. Although we will not immediately come in contact with other civilizations or beings, we will experience the shifts and the blending of the dimensions that we as human beings dwell within as we raise our vibration. As we shift, we begin to perceive things differently.

We may feel deep-seated doubt about ascending because our soul remembers the struggles of the past

The different realms and vibrations exist as the result of the law of attraction, which is the immutable law of creation. One thing that we may relate to as amateur scientists is the way in which ice becomes water when it melts or the way that oil floats to the top of water. The same laws that direct physical behaviors in atoms resulted in the formation of planets and stars, etc. Our experiences in the lower dimensions are important and they form our physical reality in the same way. However, in the quantum fields, the laws change and the phenomena that lie behind the curtain are neither predictable nor understandable to our lower selves.

In the same way that we cannot comprehend the way in which quarks (particles of matter in the quantum field) behave, it is beyond our ability to comprehend what is going on behind the scenes in the etheric realms. This is where metaphysics and spirituality come into play. A master knows where the physical world ends and where the etheric world begins and trusts in the process. When we take our calculating minds out of the equation, we experience miracles. A miracle is a shift in consciousness and it is the same energy that restores people and things to their God-given state or etheric blueprint.

Metaphysics and spirituality are the disciplines that help us navigate and connect with the creative force.

Whether working with the physical or etheric realms, we do not have control over these laws and we cannot bend them to our liking. The esoteric and spiritual teachings serve the purpose of being the bridge for humanity. They require that we behave in certain ways and then we must also learn to leave the rest to the creative force. We become co-creators in this way – we become channels or bridges. By obtaining and keeping a high frequency, we become conduits for Source energy. Spiritual teachings give us the right wiring.

We are in a time period where the understanding of our ability to create with Source energy will be the forerunner of thought until it becomes second nature.

When it gets down to the basics, spiritual teachings are

aimed at understanding what Love is. Love is the building block of all creation, yet it's meaning eludes us. I believe that it's meaning eludes us because the word Love is most often equated to the lower human qualities of romantic Love, which is conditional. Yet, we do experience spiritual Love sporadically throughout our lives. We would not be alive if this were not so.

Love created us – we did not create Love.

Love warms our heart and makes us feel alive. We feel it when we are in Love with someone, when we hold our children and pets and when we are enjoying something that we appreciate and adore. We may feel it when we are surrounded by nature or in the state of meditation. However, if we believe that special people and events are the cause of this warm and fuzzy feeling, there will then be times when we feel empty and lonely as a result of their absence. It is great that we have things to remind us of our true nature, but it is up to us to decide to stay in that space.

Love is a building block in absolutely everything that is created and there is no place that it is not. It is only our limited vision believes that Love exists in special places or under special circumstances. We go in and out of the space where we are connected to Love – that is natural for us. When we lose our alignment with the aspects of Love, we also lose our connection to Source energy. We may not know instinctively how to align with Source, but we can learn to align with the different aspects of this energy by aligning with the aspects of Love. Love is the metaphysical bridge to the magic.

Inability to feel the presence of Love has nothing to do with the circumstances we find ourselves in because it is omnipresent. It is only our lower mind that separates us. Spiritual teachers throughout history have tried to explain this to us, but it bears repeating when making reference to how we become the bridge for the new energy. Many will be challenged in the coming years to understand this concept. We need to learn to accept difficulty, challenges and losses as launch pads to higher levels of existence. There will be many changes coming and it can seem scary at first.

Who wrote the book of Love?

As a group, the human understanding of Love has evolved over time and it will evolve even more as we move into the new paradigm. It is interesting to note that Love songs through the years reflect our general understanding of this subject and demonstrate how we have grappled with it. For the most part, we have been involved in Love/hate relationships. Almost all relationships have a honeymoon, followed by disillusionment and then frustration over the loss of the initial mirage. Conversely, some of our relationships begin on a very bad note because we are mis-judging and mis-characterizing each other upon our initial meeting. Both types of human dynamics have the potential to transform into true spiritual Love. In both cases, we are challenged to learn to see differently in order to overcome these hurdles.

Love is the plan in this Universe and without it,

we are out of the game.

Many esoteric teachings have revealed the various aspects of spiritual Love. While there are many interpretations of the ancient writings found in the Bible, there are some things that are very straight forward and very clear in their meaning. 1 John 4:16 reads: God is Love and he who abides in Love, abides in God, and God in him.

In Hawaii, we say, "Akua ke Aloha", which means God is Love. Elton John wrote, "I believe in Love, it's our God." If we accept the fact that God is Love or Love is God, then we are accepting the concept that God, as a creative force is the force of Love. You will often hear me say, "God is not a man – God is the creative force of our world."

What follows is an excerpt from *A Course in Miracles.* The course uses ten attributes to describe a teacher of God, which is the same as one who embodies God, which we know as Love. These same aspects are often repeated in other teachings as well. *A Course in Miracles* is a book that serves the purpose of de-programming the errors of the imprinted lower mind. It has hundreds of pages of text, which is followed by 365 daily lessons in perception reversal. A Course in Miracles explains that only Love is real and that the rest is man made.

The excerpt is from the Manual for God's Teachers, which is a part of the course. When people say that they are living examples of Christ Consciousness or witnesses, these are the traits that they should exemplify if they are being true examples. All of the things that give us trouble in life can be absolved if we test them against these attributes.

I. Trust

This is the foundation on which their ability to fulfill their function rests. Perception is the result of learning. In fact, perception is learning, because cause and effect are never separated. The teachers of God have trust in the world, because they have learned the laws the world made up do not govern it. It is governed by a power that is in them but not of them. It is this power that keeps all things safe. It is through this power that the teachers of God look on a forgiven world.

When this Power has once been experienced, it is impossible to trust one's own petty strength again. Who would attempt to fly with the tiny wings of a sparrow when the mighty power of an eagle has been given him? And who would place his faith in the shabby offerings of the ego when the gifts of God are laid before him? What is it that induces them to make the shift?

A. Development of Trust

First, they must go through what might be called "a period of undoing". This need not be painful, but it usually is so experienced. It seems as if things are being taken away, and it is rarely understood initially that their lack of value is merely being recognized. How can lack of value be perceived unless the perceiver is in a position where he must see things in a different light? He is not yet at a point at which he can make the shift entirely internally. And so the plan will sometimes call for changes in what seem to be external circumstances. These changes are always helpful. When the teacher of God has learned that much, he goes on to the second stage.

Next, the teacher of God must go through "a period of sorting out". This is always somewhat difficult because, having learned that the changes in his life are always helpful, he must now decide all things on the basis of whether they increase the helpfulness or hamper it. He will find that many, if not most of the things he valued before will merely hinder his ability to transfer what he has learned to new situations as they arise. Because he has valued what is really valueless, he will not generalize the lesson for fear of loss and sacrifice. It takes great learning to understand that all things, events, encounters and circumstances are helpful. It is only to the extent to which they are helpful that any degree of reality should be accorded them in this world of illusion. The word "value" can apply to nothing else.

The third stage through which the teacher of God must go can be called "a period of relinquishment". If this is interpreted as giving up the desirable, it will engender enormous conflict. Few teachers of God escape this distress entirely. There is, however, no point in sorting out the valuable from the valueless unless the next obvious step is taken. Therefore, the period of overlap is apt to be one in which the teacher of God feels called upon to sacrifice his own best interests on behalf of truth. He has not realized as yet how wholly impossible such a demand would be. He can learn this only as he actually does give up the valueless. Through this, he learns that where he anticipated grief, he finds a happy light-heartedness instead; where he thought something was asked of him, he finds a gift bestowed on him.

Now comes "a period of settling down". This is a quiet time, in which the teacher of God rests a while in reasonable peace. Now he consolidates his learning. Now he begins to see the transfer value of what he has learned. Its potential is literally staggering, and the teacher of God is now at the point in his progress at which he sees in it his whole way out. "Give up what you do not want, and keep what you do". How simple is the obvious! And how easy to do! The teacher of God needs this period of respite. He has not yet come as far as he thinks. Yet when he is ready to go on, he goes with mighty companions beside him. Now he rests a while, and gathers them before going on. He will not go on from here alone.

The next stage is indeed "a period of unsettling". Now must the teacher of God understand that he did not really know what was valuable and what was valueless. All that he really learned so far was that he did not want the valueless, and that he did want the valuable. Yet his own sorting out was meaningless in teaching him the difference. The idea of sacrifice, so central to his own thought system, had made it impossible for him to judge. He thought he learned willingness, but now he sees that he does not know what the willingness is for. And now he must attain a state that may remain impossible to reach for a long, long time. He must learn to lay all judgment aside, and ask only what he really wants in every circumstance. Were not each step in this direction so heavily reinforced, it would be hard indeed!

And finally, there is "a period of achievement". It is here that learning is consolidated. Now what was seen as merely shadows before become solid gains, to be counted on in all "emergencies" as well as tranquil times. Indeed, the tranquility is their result; the outcome of honest learning, consistency of thought and full transfer. This is the stage of real peace, for here is Heaven's state fully reflected. From here, the way to Heaven is open and easy. In fact, it is here. Who would "go" anywhere, if peace of mind were already complete? And who would seek to change tranquility for something more desirable? What could be more desirable than this?

II. Honesty

All other traits of God's teachers rest on trust. Once that has been achieved, the others cannot fail to follow. Only the trusting can afford honesty, for only they can see its value. Honesty does not apply only to what you say. The term actually means consistency. There is nothing you say that contradicts what you think or do; no thought opposes any other thought; no act belies your word; and no word lacks agreement with another. Such are the truly honest. At no level are they in conflict with themselves. Therefore it is impossible for them to be in conflict with anyone or anything.

The peace of mind which the advanced teachers of God experience is largely due to their perfect honesty. It is only the wish to deceive that makes for war. No one at one with himself can even conceive of conflict. Conflict is the inevitable result of self-deception, and self-deception is dishonesty. There is no challenge to a teacher of God. Challenge implies doubt, and the trust on which God's teachers rest secure makes doubt impossible. Therefore they can only succeed. In this, as in all things, they are honest. They can only succeed, because they never do their will alone. They choose for all mankind; for all the world and all things in it; for the unchanging and unchangeable beyond appearances; and for the Son of God and his Creator. How could they not succeed? They choose in perfect honesty, sure of their choice as of themselves.

III. Tolerance

God's teachers do not judge. To judge is to be dishonest, for to judge is to assume a position you do not have. Judgment without self-deception is impossible. Judgment implies that you have been deceived in your brothers. How, then, could you not have been deceived in yourself? Judgment implies a lack of trust, and trust remains the bedrock of the teacher of God's whole thought system. Let this be lost, and all his learning goes. Without judgment are all things equally acceptable, for who could judge otherwise? Without judgment are all men brothers, for who is there who stands apart? Judgment destroys honesty and shatters trust. No teacher of God can judge and hope to learn.

IV. Gentleness

Harm is impossible for God's teachers. They can neither harm nor be harmed. Harm is the outcome of judgment. It is the dishonest act that follows a dishonest thought. It is a verdict of guilt upon a brother, and therefore on oneself. It is the end of peace and the denial of learning. It demonstrates the absence of God's curriculum, and its replacement by insanity. No teacher of God but must learn,—and fairly early in his training,—that harmfulness completely obliterates his function from his awareness. It will make him confused, fearful, angry and suspicious. It will make the Holy Spirit's lessons impossible to learn. Nor can God's Teacher be heard at all, except by those who realize that harm can actually achieve nothing. No gain can come of it.

Therefore, God's teachers are wholly gentle. They need the strength of gentleness, for it is in this that the function of salvation becomes easy. To those who would do harm, it is impossible. To those to whom harm has no meaning, it is merely natural. What choice but this has meaning to the sane? Who chooses hell when he perceives a way to Heaven? And who would choose the weakness that must come from harm in place of the unfailing, all-encompassing and limitless strength of gentleness? The might of God's teachers lies in their gentleness, for they have understood their evil thoughts came neither from God's Son nor his Creator. Thus did they join their thoughts with Him Who is their Source. And so their will, which always was His Own, is free to be itself.

V. Joy

Joy is the inevitable result of gentleness. Gentleness means that fear is now impossible, and what could come to interfere with joy? The open hands of gentleness are always filled. The gentle have no pain. They cannot suffer. Why would they not be joyous? They are sure they are beloved and must be safe. Joy goes with gentleness as surely as grief attends attack. God's teachers trust in Him. And they are sure His Teacher goes before them, making sure no harm can come to them. They hold His gifts and follow in His way, because God's Voice directs them in all things. Joy is their song of thanks. And Christ looks down on them in thanks as well. His need of them is just as great as theirs of Him. How joyous it is to share the purpose of salvation!

VI. Defenselessness

God's teachers have learned how to be simple. They have no dreams that need defense against the truth. They do not try to make themselves. Their joy comes from their understanding Who created them. And does what God created need defense? No one can become an advanced teacher of God until he fully understands that defenses are but foolish guardians of mad illusions. The more grotesque the dream, the fiercer and more powerful its defenses seem to be. Yet when the teacher of God finally agrees to look past them, he finds that nothing was there. Slowly at first he lets himself be undeceived. But he learns faster as his trust increases. It is not danger that comes when defenses are laid down. It is safety. It is peace. It is joy. And it is God.

VII. Generosity

The term generosity has special meaning to the teacher of God. It is not the usual meaning of the word; in fact, it is a meaning that must be learned and learned very carefully. Like all the other attributes of God's teachers this one rests ultimately on trust, for without trust no one can be generous in the true sense. To the world, generosity means "giving away" in the sense of "giving up". To the teachers of God, it means giving away in order to keep. This has been emphasized throughout the text and the workbook, but it is perhaps more alien to the thinking of the world than many other ideas in our curriculum. Its greater strangeness lies merely in the obviousness of its reversal of the world's thinking. In the clearest way possible, and at the simplest of levels, the word means the exact opposite to the teachers of God and to the world.

The teacher of God is generous out of Self-interest. This does not refer, however, to the self of which the world speaks. The teacher of God does not want anything he cannot give away, because he realizes it would be valueless to him by definition. What would he want it for? He could only lose because of it. He could not gain. Therefore he does not seek what only he could keep, because that is a guarantee of loss. He does not want to suffer. Why should he ensure himself pain? But he does want to keep for himself all things that are of God, and therefore for His Son. These are the things that belong to him. These he can give away in true generosity, protecting them forever for himself.

VIII. Patience

Those who are certain of the outcome can afford to wait, and wait without anxiety. Patience is natural to the teacher of God. All he sees is certain outcome, at a time perhaps unknown to him as yet, but not in doubt. The time will be as right as is the answer. And this is true for everything that happens now or in the future. The past as well held no mistakes; nothing that did not serve to benefit the world, as well as him to whom it seemed to happen. Perhaps it was not understood at the time. Even so, the teacher of God is willing to reconsider all his past decisions, if they are causing pain to anyone. Patience is natural to those who trust. Sure of the ultimate interpretation of all things in time, no outcome already seen or yet to come can cause them fear.

IX. Faithfulness

The extent of the teacher of God's faithfulness is the measure of his advancement in the curriculum. Does he still select some aspects of his life to bring to his learning, while keeping others apart? If so, his advancement is limited, and his trust not yet firmly established. Faithfulness is the teacher of God's trust in the Word of God to set all things right; not some, but all. Generally, his faithfulness begins by resting on just some problems, remaining carefully limited for a time. To give up all problems to one Answer is to reverse the thinking of the world entirely. And that alone is faithfulness. Nothing but that really deserves the name. Yet each degree, however small is worth achieving. Readiness, as the text notes, is not mastery.

True faithfulness, however, does not deviate. Being consistent, it is wholly honest. Being unswerving, it is full of trust. Being based on fearlessness, it is gentle. Being certain, it is joyous. And being confident, it is tolerant. Faithfulness, then, combines in itself the other attributes of God's teachers. It implies acceptance of the Word of God and His definition of His Son. It is to them that faithfulness in the true sense is always directed. Toward them it looks, seeking until it finds. And having found, it rests in quiet certainty on that alone to which all faithfulness is due.

X. Open-Mindedness

The centrality of open-mindedness, perhaps the last of the attributes the teacher of God acquires, is easily understood when its relation to forgiveness is recognized. Open-mindedness comes with lack of judgment. As judgment shuts the mind against God's Teacher, so open-mindedness invites Him to come in. As condemnation judges the Son of God as evil, so open-mindedness permits him to be judged by the Voice for God on His behalf. As the projection of guilt upon him would send him to hell, so open-mindedness lets Christ's image be extended to him. Only the open-minded can be at peace, for they alone see reason for it.

How do the open-minded forgive? They have let go all things that would prevent forgiveness. They have in truth abandoned the world, and let it be restored to them in newness and in joy so glorious they could never have conceived of such a change. Nothing is now as it was formerly. Nothing but sparkles now, which seemed so dull and lifeless before. And above all are all things welcoming, for threat is gone. No clouds remain to hide the face of Christ. Now is the goal achieved. Forgiveness is the final goal of the curriculum. It paves the way for what goes far beyond all learning. The curriculum makes no effort to exceed its legitimate goal. Forgiveness is its single aim, at which all learning ultimately converges. It is indeed enough.

You may have noticed that the list of attributes of God's teachers does not include things that are the Son of God's inheritance. Terms like love, sinlessness, perfection, knowledge and eternal truth do not appear in this context. They would be most inappropriate here. What God has given is so far beyond our curriculum that learning but disappears in its presence. Yet while its presence is obscured, the focus properly belongs on the curriculum. It is the function of God's teachers to bring true learning to the world. Properly speaking it is unlearning that they bring, for that is "true learning" in the world. It is given to the teachers of God to bring the glad tidings of complete forgiveness to the world. Blessed indeed are they, for they are the bringers of salvation.

(End of excerpt)

A Course in Miracles emphasizes ten aspects of Love. All of these attributes are covered in all other esoteric teachings. I believe that there are two that are missing and they are Thankfulness and Expansion.

Appreciation is the doorway that provides for reciprocating energy flow – the constant give and take that provides for constant nourishment; the breathing in and the breathing out of spirit. It acknowledges the interdependent nature of our existence and the appreciation for the interdependent cooperation.

Expansiveness is the willingness and ability to allow one's self to continually be open to Source and grow in light, depth and understanding without repreieve. We have this spark of Love in us that we have not been tought to nurture – yet we would not be alive without it. If we use it and nurture it, it expands and increases in the power to heal and create. When we come to the point where we have heightened the power of the spirit within, we are grounded, content and at peace with everything. Whenever we find ourselves misaligned with peace, it means we need to stop and observe what caused s to lose our footing. This is how we re-program ourselves to operate from a different perspective.

A miracles is a shift in perception.

In spirituality, when we talk about Love, we are talking about the ever-present creative force of Love, which actually is a vibratory field. We cannot be living and breathing without a spirit residing within us, the part that is eternally connected to creation, therefore we always have the force of Love inside of us – making our heart beat and our lungs expand with air. The integration of this Source energy varies by individual. It depends on how much Source energy we have allowed into our being. When we fill ourselves up with energy, we then become a vehicle for healing.

As a list of ingredients goes, the more of an element we put into something, the more that element will stand out. If we put a teaspoon of sugar in a cake, it will not be sweet. If we put the right amount of sugar in the recipe, it will taste right. The same thing applies to all creations. The more we bring in the frequency of Love to the energy systems in our lives, the greater the affect the energy will have on the system. Evidently, what Christ did was to wash everything with a Love so great that it transformed. We can also gain Christ Consciousness by being the embodiment of Love. We are capable of doing the same.

A little Love is better than none; a big dose of Love

becomes a miracle.

As long as we keep trying to find Love on the outside of our self and attempt to manipulate it to our own liking, we will forever find it to be elusive. We can only take responsibility for the Love that resides within us. Living in a state of high vibration benefits us personally and it creates pathways for all humans as it adds to the accumulation of higher frequencies on planet Earth.

When I was preparing to write this section of *Heaven is Here*, my inner voice kept repeating the word, dodecahedron. A dodecahedron is a twelve-sided polyhedron. Each of these twelve facets has five sides or a pentagon. Upon realizing that I was being given something that was pertinent for my writing, I stopped and realized that with regard to sacred geometry, twelve is a very important number. Some mystics and scientists believe that the Universe is actually a dodecahedron. (A group of scientists have used microwave technology to bounce sound waves off of distant places to determine their location, thereby determining their shape). If you would like to know more about sacred geometry there is a handful of things available that are very informative.

I saw the dodecahedron as a molecule of matter that keeps replicating. On its facets, I saw the aspects of consciousness or Love. While this concept is not an integral issue in this book, I believed it is an interesting concept to pass on. I DO know that Source energy has a wisdom that keeps replicating in everything – resulting in its omnipresence and eternal nature. Therefore, the closer we become like Source energy, the more able we are to be co-creators.

Co-creation has many manifestations. In essence, Source is always creating through us. There is never a moment when it stops pulsating into our being. We may however, block this pulsation of life by carrying around old baggage and wounds. When we allow life's energy to fill our being through clear energy channels, it reveals itself as life supporting words, beautiful artwork, masterful inventions, peace making behavior, or beautiful music. It may simply manifest as the smiles two strangers exchange when they pass on the street. These are all co-creations.

God is in the small things and in everything.

In order to continually expand, all of the attributes of Love: honesty, trust, gentleness, generosity, joy, tolerance, open mindedness, faith, patience, thankfulness, defenselessness and expansion must be applied to all aspects of life – self, community, society, nature and God. In order to ascend, we cannot separate the aspects of life that we choose to ignore. We cannot despise our past relationships; we cannot have disdain for the other political party; we cannot blame others for our discomfort.

There are no winners and losers in high vibrating energy systems.

When it gets down to it, everything is a lesson in Love.

How do we know what we need to work on? Whenever we feel challenged, all we need to do is check all of the angles of the facets of Love to see what we need to clean up and improve upon. Being able to be in a state of Love at all times, through all circumstances is the goal of ascension.

We control the speed at which we want to go through our ascent, but our soul chooses the curriculum.

Our soul guides us to the experiences we need as well as the challenges. Once we surrender to our spirit, our lives will begin to change and at first we may feel very challenged. This is the beginning of the undoing of our egos. There is nothing to fear and trust is needed in order to continue to move along our upward spiral.

Each day we encounter situations that test our inner peace. These things appear as arguments, disagreements, anger, frustration, miscommunications, etc. It is especially those things that come up over and over again, that must be healed on all levels of our being. All things that we heal will be addressed mentally, emotionally, spiritually and physically.

For instance, if a long line of slow traffic makes me feel so impatient that I become angry, I need to first acknowledge that it is up to me to decide whether or not to give into impatience (mental), to breath calmness into my center instead of harboring anxiety which leads to anger (emotional), to understand that everything is in divine order (spiritual) and that I can feel the tense sensations in my body (physical). Notice that patience is an aspect of Love.

All things that give us difficulty may be checked against spiritual principles in order to heal them. This method differs from the dusty old search for morality and spiritual correctness. Once we realize that these aspects are the reason for our challenges, moving through them becomes easier. Check in with your soul several times a day to see what you are struggling with.

Why does it seem that we keep repeating things we have learned?

The reason that ascension is referred to as a spiral is that we go through series of experiences designed for our individual soul growth and many find that we repeat them many times before they are fully integrated into our being. This is because there are varying degrees of an issue and different angles. Each experience is polishing our jewel.

Because the ascent requires many repeats and each spiral is different depending on the individual, people may appear to be in an entirely different place from each other, when in fact they are in close proximity on their respective spirals. People may appear to be polar opposites when in fact they are each one step away from being in a very similar position. This concept helps us to dispel judgment.

As we increase our intake of Source energy, it can make us light-headed and we have to be careful not to get ungrounded. The higher we vibrate, the more difficult it is to stay in balance. It is important to stay in touch with the breath because this keeps us anchored to our center. We need to feel our feet on the ground and stay in the moment.

This is why it is a good idea to be patient while we integrate the new energy and it is also wise to give ourselves 24 to 48 hours of integration time. The magic of higher energies is that the energy carries divine wisdom and the wisdom knows just what to do without our direction. We simply need to allow.

Whenever we clear out the old and create space for pure energy to enter, we feel better because releasing opens up channels in our minds and our consciousness, which can feel a bit as though we are becoming lighter or filling up. As new information comes in, neural connections begin to change and the brain goes through re-filing processes. This is what happens during integration. New energy is something that takes a bit of time to integrate before we put it to use.

The release and integration process will allow us to feel more intelligent, clear minded, and energetic and will improve our capacity for joy.

Case in point:

I remember going to a little Baptist church in Milwaukee, Wisconsin. I would walk into the vestibule after driving some time through the snow-laden landscape. While snow-blind, I could not see the faces of those who were greeting me, and the vibration that permeated the building was palpable. As the service went on for the next couple of hours, bliss reached incredibly high levels as the parishioners reveled in promises of salvation - singing, dancing and testifying – all with unbridled spirit, soaring so high that a mist often appeared to fill in the spaces between the people whose bodies would eventually fade in the light. Eventually, we would all have to go home.

As I drove home, I would begin to get a headache. The headache was the result of a sudden drop in consciousness as well as an all too quick grounding in reality as I perceived it to be. It would be many years before I could obtain and hold that level of bliss. This experience was my mental and emotional reference for my ultimate goal, although I did not know how to maintain through all circumstances.

Also, I did not know how to be grounded and high at the same time. I believe many people have a remembrance of a time or time period when their vibration was high. This is good because it serves as the impetus for improvement, but it does set the bar high.

It is easy to be in a high vibration when we are surrounded by other high-vibrating beings or circumstances. A master can stay in a high vibration no matter what. The way we repair our errors is to stop when we are feeling mental, physical or emotional discomfort and determine what it is exactly that we are grappling with.

When our heart chakra is vibrating high because we have surrendered, it is almost as though we are pulling the rest of our being through the eye of a needle. Once there is violet in an energy system – whether it is a person or a place – everything will transform to the highest vibration. This is a law in the etheric planes. The way it presents itself to us is that the thing that requires attention the most at the time, will surface for us to have a look. Whatever is giving us the most grief or discomfort is the issue we need to heal. Learning to ascend the spiral requires us to recognize our discordant energy and to stop, heal and integrate.

One of the most important things to understand in the ascension process is that when opening to spirit we will receive demonstrations of the power of the higher vibrating attributes and at first they will seem magical. In time, the power of spirit will just seem normal and you will wonder why you ever handled things any other way!

Higher vibrations have been tested...

I love the book, Power vs. Force, Hidden Determinants of Human Behavior,by David R. Hawkins, M.D., Ph.D. Hawkins and his colleagues conducted kinesiological studies with regard to human behavior and were able to evidence the strengths and weaknesses thereof. In the beginning of the book, Hawkins points out that most people function at or below the level of 200 on a scale of 100 to 1000. Level 200 is the level of courage. If we cannot get past courage, we are not able to move through all of the aspects of higher consciousness.

This explains why Maslow's Hierarchy of Needs demonstrates that at our most primitive and basic of functions is that of survival. Everything else builds from there. Many of us cannot get beyond this point. We need to first master survival and all of the drama that goes along with it, before we can move up. Ironically, some see survival as a given if we simply leave it be. This is what is meant by,

"Seek yea first the Kingdom of God and these things will be added unto you."

Much of what was discovered by Hawkins and his colleagues coincides with the teachings of *A Course in Miracles* and other spiritual teachings. In the karmic world, we bounce around in the lower energies and have great difficulty rising above them. If we choose higher consciousness, we need to respond to lower energies with higher energies and continue to rise up through all of the things that challenge us.

I am examining this topic because it is important to understand that the spirit has power that the body does not, and that the spiritual powers do not harm us or anybody else in the process. Instead of doing harm, the spiritual powers uplift and heal.

Once we move into the states of higher vibrations, we become spiritually actualized and able to carry out or complete our blueprints. Once we have risen above the influence of the lower self, we then enter the spheres of the Archangels and the Masters, who help us to align with our divine purpose.

Be the Change you Want to See in the World.

Where is our report card?

The most important thing to wrap our minds around

with regard to ascension is that we may only know how we are doing by the way that we feel. If we are at peace, have clarity and feel joy and bliss on a regular basis, then we are ascending.

Given that the for mentioned aspects could be considered to be a curriculum for ascension, there is a level of consciousness that keeps track of things for our benefit and that is the Akashic Records. These records are much like our cosmic transcripts. This is the place where all of our history and karma is stored. It is accessed through the heart chakra and can be read by sensitive people or people whose purpose it is to access them. Our soul will guide us through our process of ascension because it knows what we need to finish, what we need to learn and what we are here to do. This is why we must trust in our path and trust our heart. It is being brought to us by an energy that knows us intimately – our higher self. Our higher self speaks to us and directs us through a clear heart chakra that is free of anger and pain.

The Akashic Records make it easy to solve our issues because the record is unique to our personal journey through matter.

When we make a decision to climb the ascension spiral, our lives begin to unravel. There are heavenly days and there are also days when we encounter difficulty and fear in ways that we never did before. It can be a bit like passing kidney stones. The initial pain of letting go of the past is challenging and we learn that the discomfort is only temporary. Every bit of discordant energy that we heal creates space for us to be blessed with wonderful new vision and energy.

I encourage you to stay the course and to understand that it takes hundreds, if not thousands of hours of staying the course in order to undo karma and programming and to eventually ascend. The thing is – when we rise, we feel better every step of the way. When we fall, we go into depression. All who seek a higher vibration realize at a certain point that there is no way to go but up.

We don't simply walk away from our lives and find spiritual freedom. Spiritual freedom is a thing that is earned and it happens right where we stand in the now. Everything that is in our lives is there to teach us something and even if we walk away, it will find us again and challenge us until we set it straight.

Priorities...

"For the rest of my life I want to reflect on what light is...the most beautiful thing we can experience is the mysterious. It is the source of all true art and science. He to whom this emotion is a stranger, who can no longer pause to wonder and stand rapt in awe, is as good as dead: his eyes are closed...to know that what is impenetrable to us really exists, manifesting itself as the highest wisdom and the most radiant beauty which our dull faculties can comprehend only in their most primitive forms – this knowledge, this feeling, is at the center of true religiousness."

Albert Einstein

I love Einstein's reflection about living in the moment and appreciating the beauty of life on our planet. We never want to lose sight of this philosophy because it is the doorway to Heaven.

Earth and her inhabitants are going through a transformation and moving into a higher frequency. We know in our hearts that this is our destiny. This higher frequency will allow us to manifest easier, move about more freely and work with all aspects of creation more harmoniously than ever before. It is the destiny of our mother Earth to be the shining star of the Universe. As we do our work, we begin to see the benefits of moving into a higher vibration.

With our planet completely wrapped in Love, we will live in beauty, peace and harmony

With regard to the transformation, the younger ones will slide right into it and the older folks will deal with it in many different ways, depending on their DNA, their soul lineage and their willingness to change. We actually change our DNA and pass it on to subsequent generations. The work we do now is powerful and pivitol.

Either way, each bit of lightening up that we do singularly and as a group will create clear waves of energy for us to ride. With our new tools and new energy in place, we will co-create a fresh new world. Earth will become a mystery school and spiritual knowledge will be universally accepted as a norm and will be sought out by those who want to master the dimensions.

Recommended Reading:

All books by Marianne Williamson

A Couse in Miracles – Foundation for Inner Peace

Christ Consciousness Through the Twelve Aspects of Spiritual Love, by Alana Kay

The Intuitive Advantage

We were designed to be intuitive beings and to live intuitively. Since most of us were not supported from birth with regard to our instincts and intuition, we have to clear and reprogram before we are able to regain our natural state as instinctive beings. A clear mind, strong feeling center and healthy chakra system are necessary equipment. Modern day spirituality serves the purpose of teaching us these things, but I will pull all of this together in this chapter.

Life is multi-dimensional and very complex. The higher one vibrates, the more information is available and the more clearly they will perceive. The gift is developed over many lifetimes. One may be born with a substantially developed gift, yet be buried in density and ill-programming from the present lifetime. The clearer the channel is; the clearer the message will be. The higher the vibration of the channel; the greater the message will be.

The concept of intuition has been viewed in different

ways throughout time. At this time, we need to restore its dignity and recognize the necessity of engaging intuition. Depending how one has been exposed to it in their past, impressions of its value will vary as well. Some see it as an occasional blip in our consciousness, wherein we became privy to unlikely information of any variety at unpredictable moments in time. Some see it as a gift that a select few professionals possess. Some see it as a hoax. Pragmatists make light of it and try to explain it away. Still, many more fear it because fear of the unknown is a general human issue.

This section should help empower you to embrace the intuitive lifestyle and begin to trust your inner guidance and wisdom. It is possible to live entirely by intuitive guidance. At the very least, we should know it is available to us at any time when we feel hopelessly confused by the things of life and need clarity.

Since intuition is meant to be the largest part of our arsenal and is supposed to be engaged while navigating our presence on this planet, we must learn about it and learn to develop it, just like any other science. I like to think of it as putting your best foot forward. In fact, as I have mentioned before, it is somewhat like a sport, in that it requires proper positioning and it requires mastership to make proper use of it.

Some believe that we need intuition in order to predict

the future or read the minds of others, but these things are not the primary focus for those who seek spiritual mastership. The focus is on tapping into inner guidance to be used for creativity, decision making and navigation.

Intuitive guidance must be practiced. We use it and test it over and over until we master all of the aspects of it, which can take a lifetime or several lifetimes to polish. One thing is certain – only by enduring the process and being willing to make mistakes and discoveries, will one obtain this gift of spirit.

Because the balance has shifted and the higher energies of the new paradigm are stronger than the human made frequencies, surrender to the higher frequencies has become a necessity. Because the energetic pathways that connected us to the lower dimensions are closing more as time goes on, we go through a re-calibration process to align with the higher energies.

Those who are experiencing fatigue and lethargy, head fog and dizziness, lowered immune function, heart beat irregularities and a host of other symptoms are aligning too heavily with human kinetic fields instead of letting go and grabbing on to the lighter frequency that meshes with their soul. The confusion is caused by alignment with conflicting levels of consciousness as well as colliding agendas.

At this time, many are drifting around in a karmic soup.

Refusal or inability to move to the higher planes leaves one in a constant state of frustration and confusion, which often leads to violence or total shut down and disassociation from society.

During this time of re-calibration, many have integrated the challenges presented to them and have gone through the seeming voids or tunnels that lead to new horizons. These new horizons are plateaus of serenity and inner peace and a complete trust in creation and the wisdom of the soul. New avenues open up to those who are willing to allow their hearts, minds and lives to change.

Intuition 101…

Intuition is the ability to sense, discern and translate valuable information outside of the five senses of smell, touch, sight, hearing and taste. Success lies in the ability to turn down the influence of the physical senses and open up to the frequencies that are there at our disposal, primarily that of our own soul's guidance. We receive energetic signals anyway, so it is best to slow down and learn how to discern. Getting polished at aligning with the soul and rising above the fray takes diligence, patience and perseverance.

These sensations that come from non-physical or not so easily defined fields are often called subtle energies. On one hand they may be considered subtle, but on the other hand they are powerful because they are the true undertow to reality. Because the subtle energies are dominant and trump the physical, it stands to reason that it would make life easier if we would choose to traverse it with our intuitive self fully engaged. I once heard someone say, "Don't believe what you see; believe what you don't see." These are truly words to live by.

Electrical fields, data, satellite transmissions, and human activity are constantly bombarding us. To further complicate matters, the veil between the etheric and the physical is thinning! The thinning of the veil causes us to sense the tugging of our spirit more than we did before. Not only are we becoming more sensitive to Source energy, we are becoming more sensitive to all energies. These factors are actually increasing the amount of potential confusion for us at a time when we need to be getting clearer and lighter.

Consequently, during this time of transition, conditions are actually making it harder for us to re-calibrate. Think of this new energy like taking a class. The farther you fall behind, the harder it becomes to catch up. However, we must.

Because these fields of data abound, not all information

that is picked up intuitively is desirable or useful in real application, so we have to learn to sort things out and understand what we need to give credence to. This energetic confusion is creating the sense of urgency that many are feeling right about now. The soul is vying for our attention, and at the same time, we are bombarded from the outside like never before. This creates a very uneasy feeling – much like being in a pinball machine. We may find our way out of this confusion by familiarizing ourselves with Source energy as well as that of our own energy signature. Otherwise, we will endure anxiety and stress at ever increasing levels instead of riding the wave of spiritual energy that is there at our disposal – should we learn to use it.

Whenever we feel a sense of overwhelm, we need to disengage and re-center.

Initially, we may use an activity that we love, such as music, walking, running, yoga, going to the beach, driving, etc. Then, as we become familiar with the peace inside of us, we work hard to hang on to that feeling through all of our activities and encounters, and this is how we learn to be led by our spirit. The first step is to learn how to slow down, discipline ourselves to take time to smell the roses and enjoy introspection, and value this more than winning the rat race.

A strong connection to spirit is the only defense against the cacophony.

I see so many people stressing out during the day, with the goal of dousing all of it with alcohol or drugs as a coping mechanism. The desire to numb our senses becomes stronger during stressful times, yet we find that it is not possible to do so successfully, and so the cycle continues until we experience demise of some type.

When we embark a spiritual journey, it is usually because we desire a clearer, more joyful path. In order to achieve this, we need to learn to open up our intuitive channels. Unfortunately, upon opening, we subject ourselves to even more data. I suggest that spiritual seekers learn how to open up a little more every day. The increased energetic bombardment may be one of the reasons that some have started to walk this path and then made the choice to turn back and return to the rubble pile instead. I encourage those who would cave under the pressure to stay the course and go the distance. When it feels like there is no place to go – go within. Our breath and our heartbeat are the connection to our soul.

At this time however, the etheric is essentially being forced on all of us because of the increased energy. So we may as well surrender to it and learn how to re-calibrate.

The process of re-calibration begins by higher self leading us to remove karmic debris. Our intuition will initially lead us through events that need to be reprocessed and sent back out into the Universe. Each day that we clear karma, we get a clearer glimpse into the unified field, where intuition is alive and well.

Whenever we do our soul work, we feel better every day and how many people can really say that this is the case for them? Most often, humans in the old paradigm felt a bit worse every day until they ultimately died. We do not have to live this way – we need to dream a different dream. Remember, we are either in the process of living or in the process of dying. Learning how to keep our energy clear and our consciousness centered in our aura will allow us to be divinely guided from a higher source and increase our capacity for a long, healthy, vibrant life.

We will also be led into confusing and complex situations to learn how to align and discern. Learning to discern and interpret energies is probably the most important aspect in the study of intuition because without that ability we do not have accuracy and will eventually encounter mass confusion. We will "intuit" things that are useless or even part of another person's thought system if we don't know how to discern.

Whether we are born extremely intuitive or only have sporadic episodes, we still need to constantly hone our skills. Without these skills, one can become very tired and eventually ill from the onslaught. Once honed, the ability to intuit life is one of the greatest assets we can apply to living a healthy, happy, productive life in large part because it substantially reduces stress on our minds and our bodies.

It is a great feeling to be in the right place at the right time and have solutions magically appear. Tuning into inner guidance puts us in a place where the Universe can do most of the work for us.

Choosing to live intuitively is a choice to sidestep the chaos and cacophony. How much time do we waste every day, taking the wrong turn, calling or arriving at the wrong time, or mopping up after bad decisions? How often do we make decisions from a place of fear or just shut down completely because we have no idea what to do or think? How much energy is wasted debating with others who have a different viewpoint? These are some of the traps and pitfalls involved in a life enmeshed with the chaos.

Living intuitively requires us to be fully responsible for the integrity of our energy field, taking care of it just like we would any thing else. The world would be a much better place if every body would prioritize staying on center and connected to Source.

In addition to helping us navigate the physical world, intuition helps us to walk our own walk rather than to go along with the herd.

The economic crisis of the past few years is the out-picturing of misguided lives. There is no way that the government can fix it other than to get out of our way. We are the economy and we need to get back to the basics of co-creating our lives with divine will. There are literally millions of people in the U.S. right now who are going to have to start their lives over because they went along with the group mentality and all the hype instead of following their own destiny path.

The mentality in the last fifty years has been to obtain the elements of that which many considered the top six necessities of the American dream – get a good job, work hard, buy a house, drive a nice car, save money for retirement, invest, and so on. Prior to that our focus was primarily on survival. We are now being given wings to fly. We may thank those who went before us for all they have done.

Advances in technology and health sciences over the last century have increased the human capacity for a productive, healthy, long life. The integration of spiritual and metaphysical studies will be instrumental in taking us to the next level, living past 100 years and enjoying our lives and feeling good, much longer than before.

When we finally return to our spirit and realize our true blueprints, we may discover that we often put the cart before the horse when we put the big six out there as our priorities. We neglected to put spiritual attributes first. The Bible says, "Seek yea first the kingdom of God and these things will be added unto you." In the new paradigm we will feel the desire for an attribute such as peace or freedom and then the things we need to enjoy those things will arrive. We will have our material conveniences and comforts, but they will be in their proper perspective.

The problem with the dream of yesterday was that we often stayed at jobs that dead-ended us energetically and developmentally. We bought houses and cars that were so expensive that they took away our options and thwarted our flexibility in so many different ways. What happens when we get too far off course is that we almost get thrown back to the starting line to embark a new journey forward.

I do not mourn or toil when I see people lose everything to bad investments or bad weather. Instead, I see someone who has been given a fresh slate to begin anew. The good news is, as long as we learn how to forgive the past and get on with a corrected path, we will always be fine. It is a guarantee. We always get to choose again. The sooner we leave the past behind, the sooner a new life will emerge.

Expect the unexpected when re-routing.

I share the belief with many other spiritual teachers, that it is quite possible that an overwhelming majority of people on Earth could achieve exquisite connection to soul/Source. Everything would be so much smoother and substantially less stressful if this were the case. We would all begin to enjoy life and be creative and productive instead of head butting and running in circles. When we don't have to waste time and energy on do-overs, we have much more time and energy for co-creation. When we achieve this state in mass, we will enjoy a higher collective vibration, which will have countless benefits.

The intuitive channel is the same channel through which we access our creativity and genius. Where I live on Maui, Hawaii we have the most art galleries per capita in the world. Although we are not perfect, the general theme and culture is that we live Aloha and expressions of anger and impatience are highly frowned upon. We have a relaxed lifestyle here, and it is very expensive so most people here are very adept at living one day at a time because their economic status has left them with no other option. While we do have many of the rich and famous living here, most of us are here for the beauty and the high vibrational qualities of the energy and trust in the island to provide us with our physical needs and necessities.

Since relaxation and letting go are basic ingredients for the flow of creativity and intuition, relaxation and opening to spirit go hand in hand. I look forward to seeing how the talents and brilliance of humans will flourish in the coming years as more of the planet adopts many of the aspects of the Hawaiian lifestyle.

Also on the island of Maui, we are undergoing changes in our political system and many enlightened or heart centered people are running for political office. It is time that our political system becomes a vehicle for co-creation instead of a tyrannical body of corrupt people taking advantage of the constituency for their own gain. We will see government become spiritual instead of political in the coming years. I am so glad that I am in a small energy system where this concept can be demonstrated.

When government leaders lead with their hearts and intuition, they serve the people. Without a spiritual connection they only serve the needs of their selves or the few. Spirit always guides us to win/win solutions.

Being attuned to source energy and being guided is like being connected to our internal GPS and it is where spiritual power reveals itself if we keep the pathways clear. There are a few disciplines that need to be mastered in order to have a good connection to inner guidance. The disciplines overlap each other, so there are similarities. Those features are:

Discernment, Clarity, Vibration & Alignment:

When it comes to the subtle energies, we encounter them whether we want to or not, so it is a good idea to practice working with them in order to gain discernment and clarity.

I believe the best way to envision our personal energy is that of a radiant egg with the light beaming from the center of our being, where our soul initiates its streaming through our physical body via the chakras. The perimeter of this egg shaped energy is where we find the holographic field and etheric bodies. These subtle energy bodies have much to do with our communication bridge between the etheric and the physical and are part of our energetic health. Interference will cause us to lose the connection to the etheric/unified field/God.

Not only do we have messages flowing through our physical body and etheric energy, we have data drifting around in our holographic field. We also have energy cords and connections to other people. Ideally, we want to keep our energy free and clear of all outside connections and past programming.

The holographic field stores data from our experiences as well as mental imaging from others and our selves.

Our chakras also hold information that is part of our past life history as well as our current incarnation. We store the images of our childhood and past relationships and this is part of the reason that we still feel influenced by the past even though we work hard to heal and restructure it.

We need to learn how to clear our fields so that the information there does not interfere with current guidance coming from Source. While these fields are not usually visible to the human eye, this information does attract and create through law of attraction to a certain extent and does give off signals and interference because it has energy. This is why we often wonder why things seem to be manifesting I a chaotic manner even though we believe we have clear intentions. When we heal, we must heal on many different levels or things will continually re-appear.

We often are not aware of where our thoughts and feelings are coming from. When we embark on the journey of self-discovery, it is important to understand all of the energies that play/ed a part in defining who we are. Once we determine the ingredients that have become our reality, we can make changes if we so desire.

We can use imagery and breathing as well as various other energy healing modalities to keep our fields clear. Being in the sun at midday and immersing our bodies in salt water, especially the natural ocean, does a great job of clearing our etheric web and other energies. If natural modalities are not readily available, we can practice imagery, invoking colors and using our breath to clear. We can read books about energy healing or seek the help of others.

Ideally, we should know and Love our soul; we should feel like we are anchored in Source energy and that it is guiding us. We should be in touch with all of its higher attributes and feel comfortable in our skin. We should feel warm, brilliant and safe. We should be able to sit in its warmth and softness, and witness the outside world without being harmed or jarred by it. When completely mastered, this disposition gives one a full clear view of things. The greatest intuition and creativity comes from this space. Intuition increases with every bit of clearing and healing we perform.

Clearing is a long process, so expecting to take off full throttle will only slow the progress, as we must let the wisdom of Source energy help us to dismantle the discordant elements of our programming, step by step, day by day. What we do have control over is making sure that we align with our center and validate it, no matter how small it may initially seem.

When we nurture our inner light, breathe life into it and then send it outward, becomes louder and stronger. Inner guidance is like a muscle. In time, we become acutely aware of its energy signature or feeling. Ignoring our soul and internalizing the outside world is how we became dysfunctional to begin with, so it is time to change our habits. It is wise to be patient with the process and enjoy the increased benefits along the way.

As we build our connection to our soul, it grows much, just as a well attended garden does.

As we learn to identify and prioritize, we need to get familiar with the fields of data that we must contend with at all times. For the most part, we receive subtle data from:

Our mind (decisions and observations)

Our instinctive center (advancing or withholding)

The people around us (cacophony)

Our soul group (impulses, creativity and cacophony)

People we are corded to (energy, impulses and cacophony)

Electrical fields and radio signals (mental and physical interference)

Our inner guidance (visionary, audible or symbolic)

Our guides (visionary, audible or symbolic)

The Astral Planes (out of the blue, taunting, interfering, dangerous)

Countless other sources

Discernment...

All of these sources of data have a frequency or vibration. Each particle and type of data also has an energy signature. An energy signature is much like a personality in that it has a conglomeration of characteristics that make it unique. For instance, the angelic realms feel soft and uplifting and the messages are empowering, clear and supportive regardless of the content. The astral planes feel heavy, often inducing a headache and messages from this realm are often scary, pushy, misleading or manipulative. The astral plane energies are also pesky and intrusive. Very often, intuitive mediums want to hold something from the person that they are inquiring about. The energy signature is what they are tuning into and it helps them differentiate between the energies surrounding their clients.

It takes conscious, deliberate practice and slowing down to learn the discernment necessary to recognize the energy signature of the different fields and to learn where information is coming from. While I found it easy to sit down and perform a clear reading for a client, I had to practice the discernment needed to navigate everyday things in everyday life because the data in the kinetic planes is inherently confusing and overwhelming and increasing every day.

For instance, when I found myself thinking an uncomfortable thought, I would ask myself, "Where did that come from?" If I was attempting to get things done or run errands and began experiencing mental fog and indecision, I knew that I had picked up on the massive communication jam that is the mental planes. As a matter of fact, most of what crosses our mental body is coming from the collective.

When we learn to channel information from our feeling center to our brain, instead of picking up debris from the mental planes, we then begin to live a life that is directed by our spirit.

When I experience uncomfortable or confusing thinking and directions, I stop and re-center, allowing myself to begin again. With practice and deliberate intention, remaining centered becomes second nature. There is always a positive solution to every problem, but we have to seek it in the mix of data we will inevitably encounter. I don't like to block out undesired data. I like to create filters. Let's say that I have neighbors who are always arguing I can feel the tension and hear the noise. The filters I would use are: 1) They are on their own path and handling things to the best of their ability and 2) I don't believe in conflict.

We are only bothered by energy if we are enmeshing with it somehow, either by over focusing, judging or mirroring our own deficiencies. Try it out and see how it works for you. I have learned to let my soul guide me to take issue with the things I should take issue with. The ego takes issue with almost everything.

When we position our mental focus on the future or the past, or into someone else's energy, we get the clutter and all the bad news that goes along with it. Although it has long been a normal human practice to allow our consciousness to travel all over the place, it is actually one of the behaviors that keeps us ungrounded, which is of no benefit to anybody whatsoever.

Grounding is the practice of learning to be in our center or vortex and not in the future or yesterday nor in someone else's head. Doing so will yield better decision-making and give us clearer insights and answers. There will be less conflict for those who move into this higher state of being. Being connected is also the place of creativity where great art, music and writing abilities flourish.

*Intuitive guidance is the missing link with regard to
many of our problems both personally and collectively.*

As we practice working with intuition and inner guidance, we will make mistakes and that is ok. The only
way to learn how to use our instincts is trial and error. If
we need help, we should consult an experienced intuitive. Even experienced intuitives are always learning. As
we learn to normalize intuitive living, we must be compassionate and patient with others and ourselves. Even
though it is very common for a professional intuitive
reader to make a mistake by infusing his or her own
judgment or to misinterpret something, there is still value in getting a reading. There will always be bits of information that are valuable even if there are parts that are
not completely in focus.

For this reason, it is best to do most of our own work first;
this will make it harder to get thrown off by another's input. An intuitive counselor should help us when we are
at a fork in the road. We all need confirmation until we
get really strong at understanding our inner guidance.

*The abilities of intuitive mediums vary tremendously,
but this does not mitigate their importance.*

We are all in this together and we are learning together
as we go. Because intuition has become a necessary life
tool, we must get through the awkward stage. I am say-

ing this because I don't want people to get turn off by the industry because a reader was a bit off on their ability to accurately read something. If the truth were known, we sometimes believe a reader to be wrong when it is we who are in denial. Also, a client can block a reader's ability to see clearly if they have too much resistance.

The best readings happen when the querent is prepared and weighed out and stretched their own senses first. This is primarily how we learn to work with energy. We have a circumstance or situation; we ponder the possibilities, and then try to discover the clearest, most resonant answer. We release the outcome to the wisdom of the Universe and then watch things progress. If things are moving too slowly or nothing is happening in the possible streams, there may be blockages or other avenues and the intuitive medium serves as a sounding board to refine the work that the client has already done.

Discernment is the recognition that there are various frequencies and roads and it requires practice and stillness in conjunction with mindful living in order to become expert at identifying the different energy signatures of the varying fields. When we learn to be in the moment and achieve peace and stillness of the mind, we will hear the still small voice and feel the little tugs of our soul. As we master these subtleties, we refine our ability to make strong decisions for our soul journey. This does not happen over night. This is one reason it is considered a part of self-mastership. I full-heartedly encourage people not to give up on their intuition. The darkness hopes that we stay disconnected so it can take advantage of us.

In the end, we are walking away from a paradigm where others have been running our lives because we did not feel we had much choice in the matter. In order to move into an era of greater freedom, we have to come from a place of greater responsibility.

Clarity…

Discernment is part of clarity, but in order to have mental clarity and subsequent spiritual clarity, we have to be heart centered within our being. Clarity refers more to our clarity of vision and reception than to recognition of energy signatures. Our inner discipline keeps our consciousness in the moment and in our own space while our breath takes us to our center. You will notice that focusing on the breath is the focal point of many, if not all spiritual modalities.

When we take a breath in we consciously focus on our center – our starting place; our resting place. The breath symbolizes our life force; therefore, the ability to focus inward to the instinctive center is tantamount to having inner guidance and inner strength. I cannot emphasize this enough.

When we are breathing softly and aware of our breath, we are in the moment and in the core of our being. When we are in our heads, we begin to hold our breath. It takes practice to know the difference. We may be both focused mentally and on the feeling center at the same time. This can cause confusion for the under developed mind. This practice also helps us to discern the difference between our instinctive messages and those that may be flying through the ethers and coming from the kinetic fields.

Another very important physical sign of being trapped in circular reasoning inside the 'head' is clenching of the jaws or teeth. When our molars touch in the back, they trigger brain activity, which is distracting us from our instinctive center. The harder we are biting down, the more intensely we are holding on to limited thought patterns. This is one reason people have trouble sleeping. The brain will not stop processing if the molars are touching. The jaw must become loose. We need to learn to feel like a vessel and bathe in the energy of our soul in order to rest properly and rejuvenate on all levels. An active mind keeps all of our systems engaged and eventually they become exhausted and lead to confusion.

Why do people in the new age keep telling us to get out of our heads?

The mentally focused mind does not have perception;

it only has the ability to access information that it has collected in the past; therefore it ignores a large part of the information needed to provide answers for the now and beyond. It is only when we become adept at sensing and responding to the instinctive center that we become claircognizant and co-creative.

Processing, information storage and decision making in the mental planes does not engage the same circuitry as the heart connection does. Aligning with the heart connection feels different than the mental and when one is not accustomed to it, it can seem like a dream. Ideas and visions instantly appear in our mind's eye. The heart/soul projects on the mind's eye or screen and provides us with "ah-ha moments" and larger blocks of information that some may call a "knowing" or a *download*.

When we fill up our vessel and make inner focus our point of priority, it can feel a bit like we are on drugs or have been drinking because there is a loosening of the rigid constructs of the brain and logic – the same affect we seek when we use mind altering substances. In time, the brain and physical senses come into alignment and things no longer seem to be out of focus or dream like. In time we learn that the state of mental emptiness is the critical first step in attaining clarity.

Clarity allows for a directed, powerful sense of knowing

The brain should not feel heavy and tired; it should feel light and airy. Initially, upon release of the brain, it will feel spongy and confused because it actually begins to reorganize the files to be used more effectively and efficiently by the soul. This is attributed to the fatigue, malnourishment and confusion that are created by consistently maintaining high brain cycle activity. The brain, just like anything else, needs rest and nourishment. Once we detach and distance ourselves from the brain, it will begin the cleaning process. The sensation feels strange at first, but after a period of healing and re-filing, it will feel clear and natural.

On the topic of brain nourishment - high carb diets, energy drinks, alcohol and marijuana as well as a host of pharmaceuticals, rob the brain of healthy nourishment and processing. Alcohol and marijuana in particular, dehydrate the brain cells and water is critical for electrical synapses. Hydration and nutrition are critical components of cell regeneration as well. Healthy fats are critical to efficient brain function.

When we go through the process of changing our allegiance from mental to heart focused living, we are required to deliberately slow down and take hours, if not days of stillness to integrate the new energies that we are bringing into our lives. Even if we are not intending this process throughout our daily activities, our brains are programmed to do this while we are sleeping. Expect to wake up each day with more clarity.

We simply receive added benefit and maintain higher levels of clarity if we give our brains time to rest during the day as well.

Take care not to get trapped in the kinetic fields. As a group, we are connected in the mental planes, just as we are connected in the realm of the heart or spirit. The realm of the heart is the unified field where singularity of purpose and co-creative activity are born. When we go into a space of mental activity, one reason we often get bogged down and mentally fatigued is that our mind is actually joining with the postulations and mental clutter of others in addition to the misfiled information that we hold in our own brains. Then we incur the battle of the minds.

The mental plane is similar to the Internet in that there is an overabundance of information and confusion is inevitable without our center to guide us. What happens is that the ego mind runs through loops of postulations and arguments, exhausting itself in the process. Once again, the reason that this happens is that the information stored there is from the past and is generally not completely adequate for solving whatever situation we currently find ourselves in.

The brain cycle designations that we are familiar with are beta (14 to 30 cycles per second), alpha (eight to 13 cycles per second), theta (four to five cycles per second), and delta (less than 4 cycles per second). Healthy brain cycle activity for an intuitively integrated life style is theta. This may also be referred to as a hypnogogic state.

The term hypnogogic may sound like a person in this state is loopy and disconnected, when in fact the state is entirely contrary to this notion. This state provides us with the perfect balance between the physical and the etheric, allowing us to clearly observe and blend the two. In this state we can carry out great functions. When we encounter someone who is very present, very wise and appearing to be of great authority, you can bet they are in a state of low brain cycle activity and connected to their source energy.

This same concept is the explanation for savants. The excess brain activity that most of us normally have to deal with does not get in the way of the line feed from spirit where true intelligence and creativity is. If there is nothing else that will convince us of the natural genius of the soul, the existence of savants should do it.

When we remain connected to Source, our inner guidance lets us know <u>what</u> we need to know <u>when</u> we need to know it.

Oh, the tangled web we weave…

Although we may do the work that is needed to remain within the frequency of Love, we may be thwarted by information or feelings we receive through cords or entanglements. Familial groupings and life partner pairings are relationships that are more subject to entanglement or enmeshment than others. This occurs when mental, physical and emotional dynamics are interdependent, causing energetic connections between the individuals that often cause the pairings or groups to have trouble defining their own space.

Energetic entanglement also contributes to the difficulty one has when a relationship is ended as the result of separation or death. After being energetically dependent on each other for a long period of time, we lose the ability to know where one ends and the other begins. When there is a separation, there can be a sudden feeling of emptiness, almost like having a phantom pain or limb. Reality often takes a length of time to re-establish itself in our minds and in our energy. I have heard many people express that this energetic overlapping means that the partners are meant to be together and I would like to dispel that myth right now. The interdependence creates the glued together feeling, but it is not energetically healthy, nor an indicator of destiny.

As a result, enmeshment is also one of the primary causes

of power struggles in close relationships. While couples cherish their unity, a part of everybody will always fight to be autonomous. The conflict then tends to be blamed on the other person. To the end of having clarity, I believe it is important to understand this dynamic because it is a great energy drain and distractor from clarity.

Not only does enmeshment cause us to confuse our thinking and feelings for another's, we also pick up on another's feelings as a result of empathy. This occurs when we feel someone else's pain because we are energetically standing in their shoes or actually activating cell memory. Furthermore, we can actually get inside someone's head, or conversely, they can be in ours – neither of which is desirable when we are trying to be clear. We would be better off to come to a place where we don't feel that we need to cling and that we will leave it to fate to draw those people together who are meant to be together – when, why and how.

We need to take great care in handling our energy connections with others. We have to remember that any connections we have made are the result of subconscious or conscious agreements between individuals and a modicum of healing is usually called for in order to handle dissolution correctly. Working to change the undercurrents of a relationship can be like changing the rules in the middle of the game or breaking a contract.

There could be backlash if not handled properly.

I like to refer to all of this as psychic politics. I know so many people who are so engaged in psychic politics that they are unable to focus on their own lives. What we refer to as drama is often the result of this, yet the participants often believe it is normal behavior. The law of allowing helps to put this subject into perspective for those seeking higher ground or higher vibrations. If we are going to be clear about our own service and path, we need to get good at minding our own business!

I know that all of this sounds a bit fussy, but when we desire to become acutely familiar with the energy signature and the intuitive guidance of our own soul, entanglements and enmeshments are the greatest distractions we face in aligning with our soul purpose and higher energies. We were not meant to get our energy from others. We are supposed to get it from Source/God.

When we are not able to relax and enjoy the beauty of the moment and the warmth of inner self, or we feel utterly confused, it means we have interference. When we continually make bad decisions and incur accidents, we have interference. Interference is any energetic intrusion that we allow into our vortex. Each person has different sources of interference and different skills for removing interference. While one individual may have trouble getting out of their head, another individual may not be able to cease churning over relationship issues with another person.

Many people have trouble dropping the list of things to do or worrying about what others are thinking. Each person who desires inner clarity has to determine where the interference is being allowed in and work on resolving the issue so that it does not keep coming popping up when inner focus is desired instead. Often times, the chakras are jammed up from prior discordant energy that is stored therein. Journaling helps with this issue because we can isolate the problem and find a fix. Using an appropriate clearing method or seeking a reliable intuitive counselor best handles these types of interference.

We have to continually get to know ourselves and our beliefs on a deep level, otherwise we will get confused by the information that is flying through the ethers in every situation we encounter. Every moment that we engage in drama is a moment we could be getting to know ourselves and get on with co-creating instead.

Vibrational Attunement and Alignment...

Finally, really clear intuition only flows on a certain frequency and the energetic disposition of the person places them either inside or outside of this frequency. As always, this frequency is Love. The depth to which we reside in this realm determines the breadth of our vision. Translation: The bigger the heart, the greater the connection!

These are the twelve facets of Love. If you want to know more about this subject, please refer to Chapter 4 in this book or a booklet I have written which is called Christ Consciousness Through the Twelve Aspects of Spiritual Love.

- Tolerance

- Trust

- Faithfulness

- Honesty

- Gentleness

- Patience

- Joy

- Thankfulness

- Expansion

- Defenselessness

- Generosity

- Open-Mindedness

The more we are tuned into the frequency of Love, the better our connection and reception to spiritual guidance. It is impossible to connect to guidance from a low vibrating disposition.

All together now…

Breathing, clarity, vibrational alignment, mental stillness and discernment are all characteristics required in order to gain spiritual integrity. This may sound really complicated and cumbersome, but think about how long it took to learn to do things the other way. Additionally, our soul knows the road home, so when we surrender to our inner guidance, having done our part, the Universe will begin a curriculum designed just for us. All we need to do then is to surrender to it as it unfolds each new day.

Surrendering to our soul works because this process falls under the law of transmutation. This law establishes that all energy in a given energy system will eventually vibrate at the highest possible frequency that is available within it. The willingness to surrender to spirit creates a high vibration within our heart chakra and the rest naturally follows.

Our personal energy is a part of other energy systems that are all overlapping, interdependent and intermingled, yet we are capable of taking personal responsibility for our own energetic space. When we make the decision to align, everything begins to fall into place. *A Course in Miracles* refers to this as "A little willingness." Once we begin to work with the subtle energies, we discover that they are not subtle and in effect – they are actually the only sustainable, reliable power that is available to us and they will grow – eventually outshining other possibilities.

One day soon, living instinctively will be a very much validated and legitimate way to live. Also, I see a time when the subtle fields are recognized as useful tools and information by the scientific community. Then, we will be able to develop electronic equipment to do much of what intuitives are doing now, disposing of medical misdiagnoses, saving us countless millions on medical and psychiatric care as well!

At the same time, while I believe we will someday develop machinery that will enhance our ability to diagnose more accurately and without damaging invasiveness, I further believe that we will come to understand that in the truest sense, machines will never have the capacity to discern information as accurately or as in depth as a master intuitive because the layers that we have access to are infinite.

Intuition Development Exercises

We may use our inner guidance for anything and everything. As a matter of fact, we can train our minds to run through the systems of our body or the mechanics of an automobile to locate difficulties. Intuition may be used to navigate the best route to the office or to decide which foods to eat in order to maintain a proper balance of nutrients. When we get clear enough, we can receive valuable information from spirit on how to best handle our relationships. The bottom line is that intuition makes our lives much easier. We can use even the most basic activities in life to develop our intuitive guidance system.

Below are some common daily things whose experimentation with is relatively harmless and are common situations that can be used to learn how to sidestep judgment and receive clear guidance. Not only do they provide good practice, they help us become familiar with our own unique methods of working with our internal GPS.

Finding a lost object...

One of the easiest lessons in receiving intuitive guidance is to apply it to locating something that has been lost. You know the dance: you have been around the house and through every drawer eight times and you are getting dizzy in the process. What you need to do is completely forget about the lost object. Then, a variety of things may occur. Either you will be doing something entirely different when all of the sudden, out of the blue, you remember where the lost object is. This is your soul's way of letting you know where it is, but we have to get our mind out of the equation in order to get the clarity.

For those who are more instinctive than clairaudient, follow your instincts and impulses in regard to your activities for the day. And you will find yourself engaged an activity that, once you have forgotten about the lost object, leads you to it.

Because people access intuition differently, some may find that they can hone in on the item and follow an energy stream to the object. This method would work well for those who are more clairsentient. I think that this method of location requires a level of skill that most do not possess, but if it works for you, that is wonderful.

Navigating chaos...

The next time you are headed somewhere and you are late, try relaxing instead of tensing up, which is a judgment error, and then sense your inner guidance leading you through the best route. It is important to follow your instincts because they know the traffic flow and will choose the peaceful, clear route. The law of attraction dictates that if we are tense, we will find ourselves in traffic with other tensed up people. Stay calm and let the energy lead you and get you to your destination on time. Should you find yourself in a traffic snarl anyway, stay calm and your energy will likely be transferred to others, creating a winning situation for all. I use this calming energy in all potentially volatile situations and it works wonders 99.9% of the time. I have even found that by remaining calm and positive, that the circumstances of the situation will resolve themselves in a positive manner.

In this type of exercise, you are actually learning how to send a given energy out and then learning how to follow it, one moment at a time.

In a jam...

When it comes to making an important decision, we have to stop the postulations and assumptions that our brain makes. We often bounce from one thing to another, going in circles in our mind instead of stepping out of the situation and looking at it from an intuitive vantage point. As always, receiving an answer for a decision may involve either hearing our inner voice or sensing our instincts, or both.

The most compelling situation I ever found my self in was an occasion when my teenage daughter was seemingly lost. All avenues of finding her had been relinquished and she wasn't answering her cellphone. It was late at night so naturally my mind was conjuring up the worst-case scenarios. While I was out looking for her, I kept feeling a pull to go home and my logical mind kept saying that I should continue to look because I would just go crazy at home wondering where she was and how could I abandon the possibility of finding her? However, the urge to go home was strong and as I embarked on the journey I said to myself: I should know how to intuit this.

Clear intuition requires absolute neutrality – release all attachment to results.

I tried my best to relax but the fear that she was dead or in danger kept overwhelming my mind. So, I decided to accept the fact that she may be dead in order to remove this interfering thought, which was preventing my clarity. The moment I became completely accepting and calm, I heard my inner voice say: She is at home sleeping. The voice was loud and clear, but I had to remove all judgment from my mind before I could hear it. I approached the door to my home with trepidation and upon opening it, saw my daughter there fast asleep.

Once more, it was the ability to really step back and step out of the dilemma and to relinquish judgment that brought me the answer.

When the pain is unbearable...

Sometimes we perceive something inside or outside of

ourselves that other observers say is our imagination. While this is not always the case, it often happens that we are actually applying too much focus to something, causing it to become distorted. There are times when we hear a funny sound that our car is making or we have a nagging pain somewhere in our bodies and it is becoming magnified to us because we are actually putting too much focus on it. In the case of our bodies, we may also end up exacerbating the situation. Our consciousness literally goes where we put it and we have control over that to a great extent.

Spend time practicing putting your attention on something and observe what happens. Practice withdrawing your attention and relocating it to something else and you will begin to see how important this skill is in developing discernment.

Using focused conscious awareness to read a person or situation is a method of intuiting that I do not recommend. If we put our consciousness in a situation or on a person for longer than a couple seconds, we become like it and will become easily confused instead of clear. As I always say, it is best to receive guidance from our own soul.

Practice present moment awareness...

Practicing present moment awareness is probably the

most beneficial discipline for developing intuition. It requires that we have our breath calmly centered in our body, mental activity slowed to the minimum, focused entirely on where we are at the moment with what is in front of us. We can tell if we are doing a good job because we can hear everything that is going on around us and we can feel every inch of our physical body, yet we are focused on our center, allowing it to direct us.

While this is easy to do at certain junctures, it is much harder to apply to all aspects of life including bill paying, grocery shopping, conversations, cleaning, work, etc. It takes time, but with practice, one can live their life from this space. It has taken me years to learn how to do this most of the time. It comes to the point where the discomfort involved in being off center becomes very obvious. At that point, we find it impossible to live any other way.

Recommended Reading:

All books by Sandra Ann Taylor, Summer McStravick, Venus Andrecht and Colette Baron- Reid and Dr. Mona Lisa Schulz

Shining a Light on the Law of Attraction

So often, when we mention the law of attraction, we think about attracting material things. When it comes to creating Heaven on Earth, the law applies to the energy we are co-creating with Source through all of our experiences. This law helps us to understand how we create everything in our lives from our most intimate relationships, including our relationship with our self - to our relationship with the entire sea of humanity.

The old energies that supported us when we aligned with society's norms were held up by group energy systems based on limited belief systems. Because those systems were weak in comparison to the systems that will be borne of the new energy, they do not have staying power. It appears as though some are waiting for the old systems to be resurrected some day, somehow, but this is simply not going to happen because we are evolving into better things instead.

Institutions such as governing bodies, large corporations, housing, investments and others were designed to benefit those who were crafty enough to use their position to give them an advantage over others. Although these power and manipulation scenarios once worked, the have now run their course. These systems are beginning to crumble in large part because of greed and imbalance, which are metaphysical weaknesses. We have also gotten to the point where we can see the truth more easily.

The government cannot fix these imbalances – they are a result of our karmic imbalances. Law of attraction causes imbalanced individuals and systems to attract.

Without realizing it, many of us have previously been helping to support endeavors that may have been developed by and supportive of a small group of beneficiaries. Resolving these imbalances is part of the karma we need to resolve. Those who now find themselves outside of the system were likely pushed out by their energy in order to create a better life for themselves.

Also, the up and coming generations will be more aware of subtleties in human dynamics and most likely will not put up with much of what previous generations put up with. We need to become more versatile and valuable assets to the systems and the economy and then we must in turn demand that we receive our share of the benefits. All of this will play very well into the evolution of our consciousness.

As the energy of the planet vibrates higher, weaker forces lose their grip of their own volition.

I believe that we are going to see many more people develop their own version of self-employed service based on their passions. I further believe that the next generations are going to be more inclined to develop and participate in employee owned companies or employment opportunities where the management as well as the wealth is shared. I am pretty sure we have relinquished our beliefs of yesteryear, particularly when it comes to handing our lives over to a corporation and believing that our commitment and tenure will provide us with all that we need for the rest of our lives. Only a connection to our Source will do that for us.

The crumbling structures are not likely something that we personally need to address, unless we feel extremely passionate and energized by the notion and recognize that being a spiritual warrior type is in our life plan. Most things will resolve themselves. Rather, we use the insights we derive to help us get clarity and then use this information to help us understand how to make better choices. We will then see the value in realizing that we have a choice to create our own reality instead of going along with the crowd.

As the clearing of the old ways make way for the more sustainable foundations that will be relied upon in the new paradigm, we will only have the law of attraction to support us. The reason for this is, although the law of attraction has always been the law of Creation, our group egos have temporarily attached to the false and weak realities that required mass agreement in order to thrive. Since these realities are crumbling and people are losing faith in them, they will no longer be the beacon and the perceived security blanket that we once thought they were. Ego derived creations are not sustainable. Co-creation is sustainable and continually expands and replicates itself because it has divine consciousness in it.

Nothing real can be threatened.

...A Course in Miracles

Co-creating requires clarity, spontaneity and alignment with a higher vibration. This is good news and bad news because it means that we have a greater level of control over our reality, yet it puts us in the position of ultimate personal responsibility, which may be difficult for some. This is the reason that many books that tackle this subject have popped up in the last decade. These authors heeded their call to prepare us for the shift.

As we move into a freer, lighter, more evolved existence, we will tap into source energy and soul consciousness in order to be supported in many different ways. We will begin the process by learning to understand how we attract that which we attract and how things manifest. At this time, things are manifesting faster because of the stepped up energies, so we will more readily become aware of what we are creating and make adjustments more easily.

I recommend that if anyone finds their self suddenly having to live life without one of their old anchors, whether it be a relationship, job or money – or even a home – that they humble their self and start with the little things and play with the law of attraction to learn how it works for them. There is no way to start except at the beginning.

Now that others are no longer creating our reality for us, we instead must take responsibility for our creations and the experience can be a bit scary because we need to find something new to hold on to. We finally learn that we must hold on to our own center, our own vortex, our heart, relaxing and enjoying the ultimate sustainable version of security. This type of security will never leave us or lead us in the wrong direction and we can always re-center and begin again. Anything else is a distraction.

As we refine our real wants, desires and passions, we give them wings and birth new brilliant realities.

The law of attraction is absolute. This immutable law dictates the movement and manifestation of matter and has been operating since the beginning of creation. The problem many of us have with it is that we are often attracting much more than we realize and in ways that we are not aware of. We just thought we were either lucky or victims of society.

It may seem easier to deny the law of attraction than to learn how to work with it. The problem with this is that the state of denial holds the individual in patterns of blame and self-pity – many times creating a situation where a person remains stagnant or plummets in a downward spiral. Also, when we turn away from our soul's innate ability to create our lives, we become detached from our moorings and then are subject to being tossed around in the stormy energies.

When we are not sure, we may always check in with our soul – it will guide us if we are open to it.

The problem that I see with some of the earlier teachings regarding the law of attraction is that they explained that we should expect more, but didn't really explain why we often got less than we expected and often placed way too much emphasis on the attraction of material things and financial success.

Creation does not stop at our command. It marches on and we have to keep up with it. We are always creating with every thought, every emotion, and every gesture. As always, learning new ways seems difficult at first, but the new eventually becomes second nature once we embrace and understand it. It may help to clarify that we attract the events that we attract based on a few different things, many of which are not written on our wish lists or dream boards, but still important. Here is a primary list of attractor factors. After this, I will break down and explain what I mean by each one of these.

- o We attract what we are, not necessarily what we want

- o We attract what we need to complete our soul journey

- o We attract events and people that reflect the energy and information that is stored in our bodies, chakras and our holographic field

- o Through our feelings, we attract that which we love and care about

- o We attract blended realities when we are working with others

- o We attract what we are projecting

We attract what we are…

The better we know our authentic self, the more authentic our lives will be and the more honest and meaningful our relationships will be. We need to know and live our strengths, gifts and unique attributes in order for us to attract harmonious circumstances and people.

One of the outstanding features of the new age is self-knowledge and self-awareness. Sometimes viewed as selfish, it is actually a critically important aspect used in gaining valuable knowledge in the realms of improved health, and all forms of relationship dynamics. Interpreted correctly, spiritual growth should focus on what one can do within one's self in order to improve our own circumstances as well as those we come in contact with. Spiritualism should not be escapism. During the initial stages of soul searching, we spend some time separating ourselves from the flock so that we can put our personal status under the microscope.

In a true sense, any one being who makes the choice to raise their vibration using spiritual tools benefits the entire population. Because everything we are adds to the collective vibration of the planet, the decision to make a spiritual climb is ultimately an altruistic step and not selfish as some may believe. At any rate, I hope we have figured out that we cannot adequately change other people and we cannot force them to grow, but we can offer up our best self by knowing what we really are made of on all levels and building on those strengths. When we take our best self to the table, most often it will trigger the best in others. Coming from the right place, this higher vibrating force is a powerful attraction field.

Becoming intimately aware of who and what we are will help us understand why we attract that which we attract.

How do we define who we are and what we are made of? Our behavior does not define us. What we know to be true and what we have gained through experience and wisdom is an accurate description of our true being. The extent to which we have developed and integrated given traits will determine how powerful the mechanism is with regard to the law of attraction. The information and wisdom that we have integrated over time, exists as energy that is encoded in our chakra systems and this is the primary source of creation and attraction.

In our fast paced lifestyle, we take on too much in a day and as a result, fail to learn from the discomfort, make adjustments and integrate our lessons. What happens then, is that we repeat the same difficulties repeatedly, while engaging in activities to help us ease the pain and forget. The practice of slowing down, being in the moment and becoming acutely aware of what we are experiencing and creating is called mindful living.

When it comes to the creation of human dynamics, let's take the attribute of patience for example. If we believe that we must hurry through our day and push ahead of everybody else in order to get things done as quickly as possible, then we will regularly experience situations that demonstrate our expectation. As a result, this will create internal and external stress.

The Law of Attraction drives human interpersonal dynamics.

When we are behaving impatiently and aggressively and imposing our frustration on others, our behavior is very obvious. We errantly believe that if we push and cajole the clerk at the store or the mechanic at the garage, that they will deliver the goods quicker and better. If we believe that this is the only way to get things done, the Universe will confirm our belief and we will suffer the consequences as well as cause stress for others by creating an experience where the clerk or mechanic function improperly because of our interference. Everything goes wrong because we have infused the situation with strong discordant energy. If we learn instead to provide only the highest energy when working with others, we will have much better experiences.

We can choose to recognize and take responsibility for that which we are creating with our expectations and projections, or we can blame others and the Universe for being faulty.

I have noticed that when I encounter a frustrating problem with an electronic device or a product of any type and frantically call customer service, I will get a snippy, uncaring customer service person. If I calm myself down and become more patient and compassionate, I will get a rep that helps me. When we make the call, we are already making the energy connection with a similar energy as we send our order out to the Universe. We make a connection based on our projection and then the energy builds in the direction that it was intended – or seemingly unintended.

The interesting thing about blatant misbehaving is that people can see the behavior and chose to shield their selves from it or ignore it to prevent interference. It is the unseen energies that can really cause problems. There is no denying the power of the energy. Our largest influence on events comes from the energy we are feeling inside our emotional and mental bodies. When working with the law of attraction - If a situation pops up where we were feeling very anxious and things did not turn out well, we must understand that we contributed to the folly and helped create the drama.

Energy overrides behavior in creating our circumstances
– it has to be real.

The same wisdom follows that we transfer one experience to the next as we move through our lives and through our days. If we get frustrated with a computer issue in the morning and then leave the house, jump in our car and take off - still steaming over the misadventure with our electronic equipment - we will actually find ourselves encountering other frantic people on the road! Even if we just walked away from a person who was angry with us, when we fail to neutralize the experience, it will manifest again when we come across another unknowing host.

The Universe will always present us with an out-picturing of our energy, so it is best to learn how to neutralize seemingly negative experiences before moving on to the next activity in a day and in a life. When we are centered and conscious, we breathe and choose our words and actions from a place of wisdom, but when we are off center and out of energetic integrity, we invite problems and become a vehicle for all types of discordant energy to manifest into form.

We attract and then add or transmute energy in all energy systems we encounter – there are no vacations.

In addition to that which we are personally broadcasting, we will also be broadcasting energies that we have absorbed from others in our lives as well as that which we view on television. Anything that we pay attention to or bask in, will also affect our disposition and alignment. The less we give credence or sympathy to discordant energies that we view or experience, the less we will integrate them into our energy fields. It is important to have a good perspective on this.

When we integrate and embody the various aspects of spiritual values, we provide a smooth, uplifting energy in the energy systems we encounter or involve ourselves in. Not only do we benefit, but it benefits those in our perimeter as well. This applies to all spiritual virtues and facets. When we fully integrate them into our belief systems and infuse them into our daily lives, it transforms everything.

We cannot expect the Universe to deliver something other than that which we are broadcasting and projecting.

We can learn methods of clearing discordant energies that we have picked up, but it is always best to also develop means of preventing them from lodging in our energy to begin with by having proper filters. It is important to understand that every time we choose more wisely, we add to the harmonious energy fields and every time we allow ourselves to create discordant energy, we help build the dark energies that are needlessly drifting around, manifesting as school shootings and so on.

One of the significant messages from A Course in Miracles is that we affect all of humanity with every thought, feeling or action we create. We are connected on all levels and herein rests our ability to forgive and our main impetus for accepting responsibility for our creations. Just like a mathematical equation that needs to be carried out properly to get the answer, knowing how things manifest in our time-space reality is a critical step in finally solving some of our perplexing human manifestations, such as mass shootings, child abuse, wars and all forms of evil.

All pure energy that is created runs in its own stream or force field as does evil or dark energy. There are points of overlap and intersection as well as parallels. I often look upon horrible occurrences that are perpetrated by individuals or groups and find that I am not able to begin to wrap my mind around the levels of evil that are perpetrated. One day upon asking, "How could someone do this to another human being?" My inner voice answered, "A human could not do this, but darkness could." I immediately understood this based on what I know about energy transfer and movement. I know that if an individual does not take responsibility for their feelings and thoughts, their vibration can drop so low that they become a host for anything that is a match and then the individual becomes a manifestation of all of the dark thought forms that have been put out in a given energy system.

Everything that happens and everything we feel feeds into these fields and they accumulate based on their energy signature and vibration. All of the frustration and anger that we feel over the simple things in life, whether they be relationships, traffic or paying the bills – feed into a field that can consume unsuspecting hosts, such as those who have lost their will to live or have lost their minds due to drug use or the like. All it takes is a moment or a time period when one has lost their connection to Source and then they frantically get the gun and kill all of their co-workers or a group of children. The lonely pedophile latches on to the seedy and dark sexual vibration that is drifting through the ethers and can no longer control his or her self.

An individual can become the victim of a drive-by shooting simply because they just had an argument with someone and left the house angry.

Just as I have been working on this chapter, I had the chance to view the Steven Spielberg movie, Lincoln. Whether it be fact or fiction, a conversation that Lincoln had in the movie with his wife drove home an important point about the Law of Attraction. As they were riding along in a horse drawn carriage shortly after the 13th Amendment of the Constitution of the United States was ratified to abolish slavery, he told Mary that it was time for them to be happy since they had endured unhappiness for so long. The struggle to see this historic change through to fruition was arduous and he was clearly fulfilling his destiny. Was it his destiny to be murdered in the end?

The civil war, which was driven primarily by the dichotomy of beliefs surrounding the dismantling of human servitude, was deadly and horrific. In spite of the fact that he was carrying out his life purpose, which was critically important to all of humanity, he ended up being shot in the head while he sat at a theatre. How can this be? He had contributed and bore so much that he could almost be considered a saint. How do bad things happen to good people?

The raw facts are that the energy surrounding these events was dripping with hatred and violence. Unless Abraham Lincoln and his wife had found a way to step up their frequency and rise above the fray, I am afraid there would have been not other alternative ending but for him to die this way. Furthermore, he was a very humble soul and he carried guilt in his energy. He was in the wrong place at the wrong time and the energy was ripe for his demise.

What concerns me about this event and others in history is that it causes many to be afraid to step up to the plate. If one believes that they are destined to be a spiritual warrior, they must learn the proper spiritual toolset so that more karma is not created. I am sure this is what Lincoln learned in this historic lifetime.

Because we are always evolving, we can always find better ways to affect change and keep the peace while protecting ourselves.

We will always question the need for violence and I believe that we are evolving out of it to a great extent already – I don't believe we will experience something as treacherous as the civil war of the 1860's in our time, although it is not impossible. As we look upon some of the deep controversies we face as a nation at this time, I believe that we can create change much more effectively and without all the sorrow and pain that we endured in the past. If we ask spirit to be with us and guide us through difficult circumstances on a smaller scale, we will get adept at using this valuable resource and then be able to apply it on a broader scale as well.

Because of the immutable law of attraction, evil cannot penetrate or interfere with the energy of a high vibration.

When spiritual teachers talk about letting go of our story, what it means is that we have to stop judging our peers and those who are currently outside of our circles as well as ourselves. This behavior alone raises our vibration. In effect, we need to let go of many stories in addition to our own. When we humble ourselves and acknowledge that we don't know everything there is to know about people and circumstances, the door of wisdom flies open because we have removed our blinders. The Universe may then show us a solution or a better set of circumstances than that which we find ourselves in.

It is the judgment (interpretation) of our current circumstances and our projection of how we think the future should look that closes the door and muddies the water. It is law that everything must keep expanding, and moving upward. If we are stagnant, there is something blocking us and most often it is our self that is doing the dirty work. We must clean up our mess, make our bed and brush our teeth before we begin each new day and expect it to be better than yesterday. This is the law of creation. How will we choose? Do we want to continue on with the lower vibrating thoughts of yesterday or do we want to choose again and choose better?

Believe what you feel, not what you see – the feeling center is the realm of the unmanifested.

Whatever we put our awareness on will expand and grow. This is how we get stuck in circumstances that keep repeating themselves. If we put our awareness on a good feeling, uplifting, positive direction, with no pre-conceived notion of how that may occur, the Universe will paint the physical circumstances around that feeling to support it. The road to progress is not always a straight one either. We learn to trust and follow our inner guidance, feeling center or instincts. There are often detours that lead to our eventual outcomes. Process everything as quickly as possible, clean up the messes and keep rising.

The universe rearranges itself to fit our picture of reality.

A popular point of contention is money, so it is a good example. If we want to attract money, we mustn't judge, despise or be jealous of those who have money. If we think this way, via law of attraction, we will attract others who have negative feelings and thoughts toward money – all the while confirming our negative beliefs. Instead, we need to develop positive, healthy ideas around money and the people who seem to have more than us. In doing so, we begin to see how energy moves through money in a healthy realm. In order to become wealthy, one needs to see one's self as being wealthy, all the while embracing healthy thoughts around wealth and wealthy people.

As a matter of fact, if the one who thought that the wealthy people were bad, came into a great deal of money through an inheritance or lottery, the money would be gone as soon as it was delivered. Their negativity surrounding money would cause it to part quickly from their hands.

As we learn to Love everything, we must also Love money.

In the healthier matrix of money circulation, it is seen more as an instrument of freedom and a vehicle that serves the purpose of getting things done. We can only be stewards of anything on this planet, including money. There is less attachment to it here. It is not seen as a status symbol and it is not hoarded. It is seen as a constantly flowing, abundant resource that is a God given and regularly replenished. There is a great deal of trust in this realm, but one cannot enter it with the wrong attitudes.

I see so much clashing of the classes lately. I think it would be much better if both the wealthy and the poor could walk a mile in the other's shoes and stop judging each other. The clashes are karmic because both sides have money issues that are strangely similar. Both those with and those without money may be functioning with a poverty mentality. As a starting point, each would be better off spiritually to accept that both dispositions have value and meaning.

We attract blended realities…

I have observed that the single most intrusive obstacle to

working with the energies is that most spiritual seekers do not realize that they have co-mingled energies. We do not exist in a void or a vacuum. Our energy and the events of our lives are co-mingled with countless other frequencies, so it becomes quite a dance to master the law of attraction. It is a bit like a recipe in that we can fine-tune the result by adjusting the ingredients.

For instance, a household or an intimate relationship has people sharing food, beds and thought space. For those in a physically intimate relationship, virtually everything is shared on all levels. Therefore, the law of attraction can become muddy because there is more than one force creating circumstances. I have had to field questions from clients regarding their manifesting and have had difficulty helping them to understand that when they were sharing so much intimate space with another who was bitter, negative and angry, that their life path and manifestations will inevitably be strongly affected by this energy.

Because we often have blended realities, we are left with some distinct choices to make if we want to learn to work with the law of attraction.

- ❖ We may make sure we only involve ourselves with like-minded people.

- ❖ We may learn how to keep our energy indepen-

dent from those around us by staying out of drama.

❖ Do the work necessary to raise the vibration of the
   energy system we are involved in or leave.

We attract what we need to complete our soul journey…

We are being pushed to reach higher ground and it is all
for our own good. As the energy transforms, we will experience various things that may or may not surprise us.

Many issues that we thought we handled will pop up
again. We must handle them quickly and with gained
wisdom and then bless them and move on. This is the
new energy parading old issues out of our matrix. We
must take everything in stride and refrain from dwelling
on the past and hanging on. We must not begrudge or
judge our experiences too harshly. Begrudging and judging breathes new life into stressful things in the present
as well as the past and causes them to re-establish themselves in our matrix.

We need to let go of our story. Repeated patterns have
convinced us that we are defined by our past experiences. It is natural to do this, but this is a habit we must un-
learn. We must regularly ask our soul and the Universe
to show us who we really are truly meant to be. We must
constantly ask ourselves what we are creating and how
we are choosing with our thoughts, feelings and actions.

Then, we will attract new energy and be shown a way out of drama.

Relationships will appear to be more strained and issues will rise up for clearing much faster. We need to stop arguing and coercing and allow the energy to right our relationships and our circumstances with the highest possible energy. We can enhance the process by only infusing aspects of Love by breathing and affirming these aspects in to energy systems.

Ideally, we learn to attract from the soul level only and refrain from letting our egos run the show.

We must be patient while we build new energy in our matrix and allow the old to fall away. Until the time that our light body is fully engaged, we will encounter drama that is discordant or perceived to be discordant. We must not avoid things or blame others. We must handle everything with grace in order to move up the spiral. Our climb to higher frequencies will be evident to us as we view what and how we are attracting and how we feel mentally, physically and emotionally. If something keeps coming up, give it more Love. It will either go away or transform itself.

If it helps to know that historically significant figures such as George Washington, Jesus the Christ, Nelson Mandela, John Lennon and Martin Luther King went through difficulty, but were carrying out their divine mission. A spiritual path can take on many faces. It is not always a cakewalk to align with destiny, but with the right tools, it may be. Either way, we forgive ourselves for the times when we lose track of source energy. How will we steward that which God has entrusted us with?

Law of attraction shows us what we are attracting and we must take responsibility and take it all in stride

We will learn through trial and error how to work with the law of attraction. Very often, we will not be able to leave an unpleasant situation or unpleasant people because they serve the purpose of creating a framework for growth or serve to teach us how to understand how we define ourselves and make choices. In the new paradigm, we will look at things from this perspective rather than engaging in some of the general, shallow assumptions we applied in the past. Accepting the fact that Earth can be the university of hard knocks helps us accept the challenges and the journey.

As we become aware of the way things manifest, we must be careful not to believe that we can sterilize everything for our convenience. An attempt at sterilization of surroundings is an ill-fated belief system because it denies the processes we must go through and it undermines our spiritual power. For instance, if we are continually bombarded by chaos, it may serve the purpose of forcing us to build our inner peace. Attempting to move away from the chaos would stop our spiritual growth in this case. As always, close examination of soul goals will reveal the correct course of action. Also, it is better to know how to use our energy to transform, rather than ignore.

Regardless of what we believe we want, the energy will reflect our feelings because the energy knows the things that we want and need the moment we gaze upon something with desire. In the same vein, if we are jealous of the one who has what we want – whether it be fame, freedom, peace or a nice home- we will not manifest it. We manifest what we need and Love.

In addition to taking responsibility for the events of our day, there is also the concept of how we perceive the events. We may believe that we are having a bad day or having unpleasant encounters, when in fact, we are encountering circumstances that serve the purpose of helping us to grow mentally, spiritually and emotionally. I noticed that truly positive people see challenges as opportunities for growth.

Fortunately, if we consistently give everything our best and reach for higher ground, seemingly difficult events occur less often because we don't need them as much. Additionally, accepting that difficulty is often a feature of density and life on Earth helps us to take everything with a grain of salt, helping us to refrain from internalizing things too much. The challenge lies in knowing if the difficulty is self- created or a gift. This can be challenging.

When we feel we have relinquished all of our best thinking, it is time to say, "God's will be done." This should effectively correct all courses.

Recommended Reading:

Ask and it is Given, Series by Esther and Jerry Hicks, The Teachings of Abraham

All other books by Esther Hicks/Abraham

All books by Stuart Wilde

Stairway to Heaven

O ur purpose and our happiness are one in the same...*A Course in Miracles*

Our individual and society evolutions can be viewed as a spiral or a climb. So, how are we doing? We have developed ways to quantify and analyze just about everything. We use economic indicators such as housing prices, employment figures and the consumer price index. Some believe that a huge national deficit is bad, while others believe it is no issue. We have tried to find ways to determine what is normal for humans and how to accurately analyze an individual's circumstances. How do we really determine how we are doing as a group or as an individual?

As humans, we have been through much, especially in the last few hundred years wherein we have experienced a huge acceleration. The technological advances that afford us the freedom and ease that we now enjoy are indicative of our advancing consciousness on the deeper levels. As our perception of time speeds up and technology catches up to spirit, we accelerate even more. So many of us feel crushed under the pressure of daily life, which is bringing all of our karma to a close in order to enter the new paradigm, fresh, re-energized and ready for a new way of living. Although life should be getting easier and less stressful, we often find ourselves confused and frazzled instead.

The exhaustion we are feeling during this crunch time will bring many to their knees and will also become the undoing of many as they succumb to diseases and fear. Some will perceive this time period as scary and uneasy, while others will see the opportunities to let go of outdated thought systems and move into a higher frequency. Those of us who see things in a positive light need to step up to the plate and educate and position ourselves according to our soul's design in order to be of assistance to those who lag behind, for they will need us to show them the way.

The restoration of many of the ancient healing modalities that recognize the connection between thought, emotion and behavior and physical/mental disposition is going to be crucial. It is here that we will find the answers that we seek. We must begin to see the human body as the storehouse for spirit and listen to its language and its signals. These sciences are gaining support in general and are beginning to encroach on the field of neuroscience – a trend that usually results in full recognition in mainstream thought. It will be much needed as we move into the next stage of human evolution.

The physical body is our navigator and our barometer

Because the human body is an energy map and an out-picturing of the soul, it serves as the sounding board for the spirit and it is used by the soul to help the earth self navigate planet Earth. We have to also take care of physical self and stop force-feeding our bodies junk food, pills, drugs and other poisons. It is easy to understand that one cannot achieve physical peace without taking care of our body and our minds. We gain mental and emotional peace when we align with Source energy – there is no other way. Pills and excuses do not work in the long run.

Change can seem painful at first and the new energy mandates that we streamline our ability to move through life's seeming challenges by accepting them in a positive light and allowing them to teach us and move us upward. Avoidance and judgment will keep us locked in lower frequencies. There is no escape from the work that must be done and the rewards will be greater than we can imagine. As more people step up their frequencies, there will be exponential growth on our planet.

There is a disease caused by a genetic anomaly where

the host does not feel pain. At first glance, it seems like it would be a great thing to live without pain, but the children who have it end up injuring themselves sometimes severely and in one case a child actually dug their eye out of the socket. I am sorry if this sounds gruesome, but I need to emphasize the fact that the body lets us know when things are wrong through discomfort and pain and it is purposeful. Discomfort and sometimes pain is how the soul gets our attention.

If we took away the numerous boundaries set by the physical body, the results could be catastrophic. There is a possibility that some of the spiritual prophecy and scientific projections with regard to drug resistant diseases will come to pass and we will have only the energetic healing practices to fall back on to pull us through.

When we learn to live by the true laws of metaphysics, there will be nothing that can stop us. In the meantime, we are sheep being controlled by the system.

Living as a spirit in a limited human body can seem restrictive at times, but it serves a purpose. We have been limited because we would not have used our power in a responsible way. We will now receive more light as we use it responsibly and for the benefit of all humans. The higher energy, if accepted and channeled by the right amount of people, used in the right way, will not allow these prior levels of evil and destruction as we experienced in our history. Evil and malfunction cannot live when flooded with light.

It is our purpose to commit our lives to becoming an energy bridge

If we do not accept full responsibility for this function, we continue to blame others and in the end, we blame God. God is Love and God just is. It is up to us as extensions of God to decide how we will create – each moment and every little thing.

I often hear references to people who are battling cancer and I have to wonder, why would you want to battle something that is in your body? Only Love heals. We need to Love our lives and our bodies back to health. We also need to Love this planet and its inhabitants back to life. Yes, sometimes we have to be the spiritual warrior, but that takes a special skill set which can be learned. We must learn to educate those who would oppress the light and spirit of others in a way that is palatable to many.

We must balance the resources and the playing field through diligent, persistent, educated karmic resolution and stop expecting the government to do it for us. We do this by handling that which is in front of us at the moment. When we get good at those things close to the hearth, spirit may advance us to a level where we can influence larger groups of people. In the meantime, to dwell on all that is wrong would be counter-productive.

We must also embrace patience. We need to look deep inside and stare the truth in the face in order to create real change. We have a society norm that has conditioned us to want the quickest fix. As a result, we have created much that is not sustainable and I believe we are going to get tired of hearing this, but sustainability will be the goal of many energy systems now. The days of the disposable society need to end. The old way is stressing us out and making us sick and resistant to healing.

Our overuse of antibiotics is creating superbugs. So many of us are becoming acutely aware of the fact that the pharmaceutical industry is putting profits over health, duping us into using drugs with sometimes crippling side affects to treat our maladies rather than addressing the cause and holistic cure for our issues. However, holistic healing requires honesty, patience and humility.

We are essentially doing the same thing when we over legislate and continually ask the government to control us and take care of us. Once again, it is the quick fix. Instead of doing the real work and having the real discussions head on, we turn things over to the government. This has gotten us nowhere. Real evolution comes from people creating change. Government cannot do this for us.

Not only do we take drugs that we often do not need, we allow things to fester on a personal level and a societal level. The physical world is the out-picturing of that which needs to be addressed on another level. All we need to do is take a look around and it is easy to see that much needs to change before we can rest easy and look upon a job well done.

Our government, economy, and eco balance are entirely out of sync with energetic reality that things are going to keep snapping. Each of us must know what are job is with regard to the reconstruction of this planet.

When people wake up to their true identities and integrate their true role, our societal issues will begin to fade

We are being led by false leaders who are power hungry and greedy. At the same time, all the legislation and government reform in the world is not going to fix things for us. We can no longer continue to sweep things under the rug and put Band-Aids on things.

As long as we look around and see rampant crime, neglect, poverty, depression and anger, we have work to do as a society on levels much deeper than handing out aid or enacting laws. These issues are indicative of our imbalances and inability to access the spiritual realms and in many cases are the responsibility and creation of many, therefore requiring complex and innovative solutions.

When people try to blame one leader or one political party, or one rich person, then they are seeking a scapegoat and we must stop this behavior. We must first look at the man in the mirror and then we must open our minds and hearts and apply a huge dose of compassion to all humans, from the desolate to the privileged, and do whatever it is that must be done from our own perspective to begin to create better ripples in the pond of humanity.

What applies to a singular home also applies to a town, a city a state and a national government. We need to clean up all of our energy systems and I am sure that there are people out there, hanging around in the weeds, who will be willing to put on their light worker hat and accept the piece that is theirs to illuminate. Hopefully soon, we will begin to see this and accept this and get to work on creating a world that is appropriate to house the spirit beings that we are.

As we learn to co-create, we will provide a new space for our dear and precious indigo, crystal and rainbow children to thrive. Until then, they will probably continue to spend too much time watching TV, eating the wrong food and getting into trouble. There is nowhere for them to go until we clean up the pathways.

We as individuals, a society, a country and a planet are evolving on many fronts, but it takes time and patience and many must be willing take a risk and do what they came here to do.

Spiritual growth is measured by the ability to house, integrate and dispense source energy

All of the events in our lives, no matter how they originated, serve the purpose of helping us to grow spiritually. We may not have to know completely the reasons for all of our relationships and occurrences in our lives, but we must always do our best and not give up when we are presented with something we perceive as difficult. I have had many things come into my life that seemed difficult at the time, their contribution to my growth was not evident at their inception, and their beneficial nature not yet revealed. In retrospect I would not have traded them for anything else.

If we consistently do our best in every situation we find ourselves in, we can be assured that we will continue to grow spiritually. When we learn to stop judging circumstances as good or bad, we improve our ability to see the benefit of the circumstances and then we gain from our experiences by allowing them to propel us to the next level.

A relentless amount of patience is needed in our climb and I want to emphasize that it takes time to come into the clear. It has been said that it takes a full 1000 days of being completely centered and grounded in our spirit to birth a new reality for ourselves. It may sound daunting, but the nice thing about the climb is that it rewards us every day with renewed energy, increased joy and continually clearer focus.

At a certain point of attainment of spirit, one begins to feel as though life is heavenly – experiencing Heaven on Earth.

Because much of the earlier teachings stressed the obtaining of objects of desire, we forgot that the greatest level of attainment is that of the spiritual realms. The fascinating thing is that as we raise our vibration and our ability to store source energy, our ability to manifest the things we need and desire becomes much easier because our life force is stronger – sending out stronger signals with larger returns. This is what is meant by the Bible phrase, seek ye first the Kingdom of God and these things will be added unto you. Those who embraced spirit in the past millennia were forced into secrecy because the false powers were jealous of their light and their ability to manifest. The light bringers must no longer hide and be silent. We have developed a habit of hiding our light because of past oppression and this no longer serves anybody on this planet.

When we are having trouble manifesting things we need, we must increase our vibration

The clarity of our mind, the lightness of our body and the joy in our hearts become our way of measuring or quantifying how we are doing on our journey. In this space, we also touch eternity and gain great intuition and vision. When we are in a place of clarity, it is easy to see the next step in our lives and then we can open the doors of opportunity and abundance as we feel things approaching. At this point, we are much more than a simple human – we have integrated our divine presence into our daily existence and no longer have a fear of the unknown, nor do we have a fear of death. We have come to the point where we feel our energy as it goes out before us and leads us, trusting every step along our journey and loving every moment of it.

Mindful living and appreciation of all things, great or small...

The new age encourages us to open up to our greater selves, which brings about epiphanies and flashes of brilliance. Great new things begin to occur in our lives and it can be tempting to become bored with the seemingly mundane aspects of life. A word of caution here: we become ungrounded when we loose track of the moment and loose sight of the little things. If there is anything that we should take from spiritual teachings, it is that God or creative force is in everything and that there is no place that God is not. If we lose track of the small things and forget to find joy in all processes, great or small, then we will find ourselves going way off track.

Without being aware of our breath and without being completely in the present moment in a state of appreciation and acceptance, we will not be able to take advantage of the new energies. This state I have just described is what is known as grounding – the proper wiring that connects us to both the Source energy and earth frequencies adequately enough to be anchored, propelled and guided.

When we stand clearly in our vessel and remain in the moment, we experience what is known as mindful living. Not only is this the only way to have the law of attraction truly work full force, it is advantageous because every moment comes alive, as it rightly should, and this is an absolutely wonderful way to live. Every moment and every action of our lives shine with divine energy when we allow ourselves to cherish and appreciate even the smallest of things – the smell of the dish detergent, the sound of the water, the feeling of a breath coming into our lungs, the glisten in someone's eyes.

Each moment is a miracle, propelling us to the next step

on our path. There is not a little thing that does not matter and blessed is he who can see this. When spiritual teachers encourage us to let go and let God, present moment awareness and appreciation is the vehicle through which we become aware that every moment is a miracle and that the specific things that we believe we are wishing for no longer keep us in a holding pattern while we wait for them. We are no longer waiting – we are living every moment. In this place, we also know and sense what is coming our way.

We cannot wait around for things we wish to have happen. When we do so, we put ourselves into a void. A miracle is being delivered in every thing and in every moment, most often leading us to the manifestation of our desires. The refusal to see this will negate the arrival of those bigger things that we believe we want and need – the house, the car, the job, and the relationship.

When all is said and done, the law of attraction requires us to be deep in our feeling center, connected to Source energy, and in the moment. From this place we attract our life instead of planning it, we don't have to fight with others because we are no longer pitting ego against ego, and we are allowing the perfect plan to evolve for all things, taking correct action when necessary.

This excerpt, which is the epilogue from *A Course in Miracles*, provides thoughts to nurture a sense of deep inner peace regarding the restoration of our true lives:

This course is a beginning, not an end. Your Friend goes with you. You are not alone. No one who calls on Him can call in vain. Whatever troubles you, be certain that He has the answer, and will gladly give it to you, if you simply turn to Him and ask it of Him. He will not withhold all answers that you need for anything that seems to trouble you. He knows the way to solve all problems, and resolve all doubts. His certainty is yours. You need but ask it of Him, and it will be given you.

You are as certain of arriving home, as is the pathway of the sun laid down before it rises, after it has set, and in the half-lit hours in between. Indeed, your pathway is more certain still. For it cannot be possible change the course of those whom God has called to Him. Therefore obey your will, and follow Him Whom you accepted as your voice, to speak of what you really want and really need. His is the Voice for God and also yours. And thus He speaks of freedom and of truth.

No more specific lessons are assigned, for there is no more need of them. Henceforth, hear but the Voice for God and for your Self when you retire from the world, to seek reality instead. He will direct your efforts, telling you exactly what to do, how to direct your mind, and when to come to Him in silence, asking for His sure direction and His certain Word. His is the Word that God has given you. His is the Word you chose to be your own.

And now I place you in His hands, to be His faithful follower, with Him as Guide through every difficulty and all pain that you may think is real. Nor will He give you pleasures that will pass away, for He gives only the eternal and the good. Let Him prepare you further. He has earned your trust by speaking daily to you of your Father and your brother and your Self. He will continue. Now you walk with Him, as certain as is He of where you go; as sure as He of how you should proceed; as confident as He is of the goal, and of your safe arrival in the end.

The end is certain, and the means as well. To this we say "Amen." You will be told exactly what God wills for you each time there is a choice to make. And He will speak for God and for your Self, thus making sure that hell will claim you not, and that each choice you make brings Heaven nearer to your reach. And so we walk with Him from this time on, and turn Him for guidance and for peace and sure direction. Joy attends our way. For we go homeward to an open door which God has held unclosed to welcome us.

We trust our ways to Him and say "Amen." In peace we will continue in His way, and trust all things to Him. In confidence we wait His answers, as we ask His Will in everything we do. He loves God's Sin as we would love him. And He teaches us how to behold him through His eyes, and love him as He does. You do not walk alone. God's angels hover near and all about. His Love surrounds you, and of this be sure; that I will never leave you comfortless.

(End of *A Course in Miracles* Excerpt)

The planet is waking up from a deep sleep.

Don't be fooled by the tricks the darkness is playing

in order to distract us.

The journey to the true self is the journey back home – to Heaven. We don't have to die to get to Heaven and it is not somewhere else – it is right here in our hearts. Those who wish to carry the light of God must be willing to transform everything that is presented to them and continue to shine through all of the darkness. It is not a matter of putting on enough protests, or creating more institutions or laws. It is the realization that we don't need to fight the darkness – we just need to shine a light on it.

No body can force us to live a heart centered life. It is an intentional, personal choice. When enough people on the planet make the decision to carry the light, the entire world will be transformed, and this is what a rapture is.

Just like Dorothy in the Wizard of Oz, who discovered that in order to go home – all she had to do was click her heels together. The answer was there all along.

Recommended Reading:

A New Earth by Eckhart Tolle

Whispering Winds of Change by Stuart Wilde

About the Author

Having grown up in a typical American family, I have struggled all of my life to blend the very esoteric me in to a world of form where everything I am seems to be going against the grain. The pull to be myself has always been stronger than the pull to be like the crowd, yet I have consistently remained enmeshed with the people and structures of modern society, closely observing and constantly playing with the dynamics and the energy – trying to find ways to make it palatable – a state which some refer to as, being in the world, but not of it.

I have had my ancient eyes open since I can remember, but have had to be patient while more has been gradually revealed to me over time as I have moved through challenges and deepened the connection to my soul.

I am about to describe many of the hardships and challenges I encountered in my growing years because I know that most people have to deal with a great deal more than most of us realize.

From a very young age, I was already aware that I was

an intuitive medium. All people who are sensitives or energetics are aware of this fact early in life because they are visited by spirits, are very sensitive to energies of all types and are hyper-aware of human behavior on a deep or spiritual level.

I spent countless hours awake every night trying to hide from the spirits that appeared in the night and alternatively spent many hours contemplating the deeper meaning of life until the wee hours of the morning. I often heard words of wisdom that seemed to be coming from a being that was resonating with my own being. I have since come to understand the complex metaphysical phenomenon that manifests as this wise resonance. It is the field of Christ Consciousness and my soul is connected to it through quantum entanglement.

Because everything is electromagnetic and connected through quantum entanglement, the higher realms of consciousness became available to me when the world was quiet and my mind was still. Because I always felt close to Christ Jesus, I believed this resonance to be him, although it was actually Christ Consciousness - the realm where ascended beings exist. This realm is omnipresent because it is of the highest vibration.

Because I was open and sensitive, lesser spirits also taunted me. When I was younger, I dreaded the night. By learning to receive answers from the masters, create filters and keep a consistently high vibration, I no longer dread the dark or the night; I sleep very well as a matter of fact. I did have to work on things and it required a commitment and investment of time.

I was gangly, skinny, knock-kneed and shy and felt very awkward in my earlier years. I spent the first couple years of my life in leg braces because my hip joints were severely out of alignment. My family was poorer than most and my clothes were hand-me-downs. All of this made me feel very self-conscious and the children who

were my peers made it painfully obvious that I was indeed awkward and different. I was picked on and told by my mother to turn the other cheek, which made me feel as though I should not defend myself. The things we are told when we are young become our programming because it is all we know when we are new to the world.

Everything about me made me feel like an outsider and I was very disempowered. The home I grew up in was full of stress. I suffered headaches from a young age and always felt agitated and physically and mentally uncomfortable. I fought short bouts of depression and was an insomniac until I set out on my own at age 18, when I was more able to be my true self and be freer.

Given that I had a very spiritual bent from the beginning of life, growing up surrounded by an atheistic family was one of the first challenges I remember having to deal with. As the family member who felt all the pain, I was subject to outbursts because all of the stress and pain was internalized by me. Because of this and because I was different, I was labeled the black sheep - a projection that took me many years to correct in my own mind. Since most families seem to have a black sheep - the one who challenges everybody's reality - one has to wonder if this is part of a divine plan.

Many older souls become alcoholics and drug addicts, depending on the level of dysfunction that the given family suffers. I escaped the path of the addict, even though many in my birth family are alcoholics.

In my earlier adult life, I attracted people who brought reenactments of my familial relationships. I discovered as many other have, that all of my childhood memories were lodged in my holographic field and mental patterning, causing the drama to play out in my life over and over. Our past remains in our attractor field unless we clear it out.

My familiy relationships also played a role in my development of self-karma. I grew up with an undue amount of criticism and competition, which fueled a belief that I needed to prove to the world as well as myself that I was OK. This made me over achiever and a perfectionist. Perfection was my way of making sure that I would not endure criticism or complaints, and this quest for perfection is forever elusive because it is not truly attainable in the physical world.

As a result, the world became a reflection of my own beliefs. The interesting thing was that the closer that I got to perfection with things, the more I found myself having to endure criticism! I was attracting other perfectionists – for whom nothing was ever good enough, regularly confirming my inner beliefs, so I had to constantly seek higher levels of perfection in the hope that one day everything would be up to par with my impossible standards. One way that I found to correct my perfectionism was to strive for excellence and let Spirit handle perfection.

This type of imbalance is very common in our human experience and with intuitive introspection and careful spiritual analysis, we can re-arrange all of our past patterning and past experiences the same way. All of the information from our history is in the Akashic records. Because of our soul history and innate personality, we all experience and assimilate things differently.

My extremely inquisitive nature, much like that of today's indigo and crystal children, resulted in a general disposition of boredom with everyday life, and still does to this day. Seeking solace and adventure, and as young as seven years old, I gravitated to the neighbor- hood churches whose doors were open to the public in 1960's. I felt a deep level of peace in these holy places and I felt a sense of belonging there that I did not feel at my family home.

I felt a connection to Spirit for the first time, standing alone in a Catholic church. Familiar but indescribable feelings of bliss, depth and contentment rose seemingly out of nowhere. The vigil candles flickering in the corner, the lingering scent of frankincense and myrrh, and the stillness and the stature took me to a place inside of me that was entirely different than the one that had been projected on me by my family and my peers. Swaddled inside these hallowed walls, I longed to be of service to God and often envisioned myself as a nun, priest or monk.

The thought of living a life of devotion to spiritual matters has always intrigued me. In reflection, this makes sense, since I have discovered through meditation that my soul history that of the Order of Melchezedek - an eternal priesthood. The Order of Melchezedek are souls that always dedicate their lives to the spiritual advancement of humanity and always incarnate to be of service.

In this lifetime, I have had to find ways of weaving my soul into normal every day circumstances. It is possible to do so, but requires a high degree of mastership. I am sure that in past lives I lived in monasteries and such, where living in connection to spirit was the norm. Spiritual pursuits, especially at this point in our evolution do not have to exist solely outside of the grind. I see the benefit of this and I hope everybody else does, because this is the time for all of us to bring our special offerings to the table of life. I see the day when corporate America embraces spiritual teachings to improve business.

Bits and pieces of information came in to me over the years and some of them have stood out in my memory. I had moments of epiphany that would yield small fruit and then be put on the shelf until a later date. There were not any existing avenues in my mind or in my environment that would support any further adventure. Al- though I usually felt it was par for the course; there have been many times when I felt trapped in this low vibrating society.

These days, there is so much available for the spiritual seeker. With the proliferation of spiritual literature and the Internet, no stone should remain unturned.

Beyond our fears lay our greatest treasures.

Having to fuel my own desires and ambitions from an early age made me the self-starter that I am and I am thankful for this. While I once begrudged the fact that I did not have a fairy tale childhood, I now find that having to find my own way and having to be my own parent and life coach was actually a good thing.

My early teen years were a very pivotal time for me as I found myself filling my lone time with more useful pur- suits, rather than filling them with feelings of emptiness and loneliness as I did in my earlier youth. I spent time reading and writing, developing a relationship to music and simply gazing out the window, looking for meaning. I began the lifelong process of self-discovery during those quiet moments in my bedroom and my creativity was born.

We all choose our parents for various reasons. Understanding the reasons is a big part of our healing. I am clear on some things, but the jury is still out on the others. However, it is now a moot point now, since visiting hauntings and performing clearings are some of my fa- vorite things to do. I find the field very exciting, though it is not my professional focus. My professional focus is helping people find a connection to their soul and pur- pose.

Heaven on Earth...

As I lay awake late at night, my radio alarm clock would make a clicking sound when the numbers 11:11 made an appearance. A chill would run through me each time and something inside of me knew it bore significance. Through the years, I have met others who experienced the same thing, one of whom was my youngest brother. Although we all felt it must have significance, we did not know what it was.

Around the same time period, which was in the early 70's, I was perusing my Bible and came across a phrase that said that one day, Heaven and Earth would be as

one. Upon reading that statement, I paused and imme- diately felt that the appearance of the 11:11 had something to do with this, as though spirit was trying to communicate something with me. My next thought was that the merging of Heaven and Earth would occur in my lifetime. Although this rang true to me, I passed it off as a wild imagining. That was too big of a thought for someone like little old me to conjure up.

I mention these things because I feel we should trust those things that come to us in moments of inner clarity. These are things that are coming from the unmanifested.

It would be more than 20 years later that these realizations would begin to make sense to me. With the proliferation of the spiritual new age, others have risen up and proclaimed that this is the time when the Earth will be restored to its natural state, which is Heaven on Earth. There are also millions of results on the internet when one searches 11:11. Those moments I had when younger were now being validated.

I was actually in a state of meditation at many times, without realizing it. I was tuned into the cosmos, making discoveries that would come to light much later in my life. Nonetheless, spirit continued trying to communicate with me even though I was not yet ready to listen. The connection to my soul now became a much higher priority than it ever was.

In retrospect, I have noted that these openings began to occur in a group during a time when my lower self was once again completely exhausted – leaving an opening for my spirit to resurface. I consulted spirit medium, Anne Marie of Milwaukee in an effort to find some meaning in the events that were unfolding and all she could say to me at that time was that it was my life purpose to be a spirit medium and that the light of God shined through me. She didn't have much more to say - the rest was up to me to discover. Nobody had ever said anything like this to me and it struck a nerve. The pump was primed and my life began to move in a different direction, creating the opening for more synchronicity and etheric help.

Eventually I came to understand that my Love of Spirit and my open and willing heart actually emitted a light, which is a healing energy. Before I understood this, I was easily taken advantage of and used by others. It was time that I learned what God's plan was for this energy. Events began to pull things together for me an accelerated as time went on.

While working at a client's home where I was installing wallpaper, the homeowner began asking me probing questions about my philosophy of life. After a long list of questions, she squarely asked me, "Where is Heaven?" I turned around without answering and looked at her and she said, "It is right here." We ended up talking for hours and eventually discovered that she also frequently saw 11:11 on the clock and knew it had spiritual significance.

We parted that day committed to determining what the

meaning of 11:11 was and indeed we were introduced to a book called 11:11, Inside the Doorway by Solara. We were not alone. There was a clear connection in the unmanifested and we all knew it had heavenly connotations.

My soul had been trying to communicate with me all my life and I was finally ready to listen. The soul gives us nudges and waits patiently for us to give it permission to forge on.

My psychic channels having been opened wide as a result of these events. I began to become more open to my sensitivity to energies again, and began to know who was calling when the phone rang and so on. Right around the same time, I was incurring a gradual emotional breakdown as repeated mentions of horrific crimes in metro Milwaukee threatened my vision of humanity and the safety of my young children.

I always had a tendency to be empathetic largely because I see all of humanity as one being. I feel the pain of others and take things very personally. Also, many people that I knew had been passing away at an unnatural pace and one Friday afternoon, I broke down and began to cry because it was my last resort to relieve the tension and frustration I was feeling.

I rifled through the Bible and prayed to Jesus, trying to find an answer and could not. I so believed in the goodness of God and the goodness of mankind, yet I was being repeatedly disappointed and horrified by what I was experiencing.

I know that many others have felt the same way. How could a good God let bad things happen? A good man that I had just met and knew for a brief period of time had just passed away – a loving husband and father of an adorable baby boy. I desperately needed to know why mean people survive to perpetrate such dastardly deeds while good people perish? Little did I know that my understanding of spirituality was about to take a huge leap.

At the time, I did not know why, but the crying was feel- ing very warming and good as I went deeper into my being. Actually, tears are cleansing and they cause a re- lease of feel good chemicals. I felt enveloped by Love and began to realize many things that had gone unanswered for me in my life. I did not try to stop the tears because they felt good and decided to see where they would lead me. With tear filled eyes, I stood in line at the grocery store and saw a beautiful face on the front of a paperback book: A Return to Love by Marianne Williamson. I still remember the moment I discovered it and it looked like a mirage at first.

I knew this book was for me and as I read it, the self that I had buried and left behind so many years ago began to come back to life. I subsequently obtained my copy of A

Course In Miracles, which was the book that motivated Williamson to write *A Return to Love.*

Up until this point, I had lost track of much of who I was when I was younger and these two books played such a large role in helping me return to my true self. As a young adult, I finally realized the Love had been benched for me because I did not know what to do with it. I knew that the answers that I needed were in that text and the day I finally opened up to the first page was the first day of the rest of my life. The introduction reads:

"This is a course in miracles. It is a required course. Only the time you take it is voluntary. Free will does not mean that you can establish the curriculum. It means only that you can elect what you want to take at a given time. The course does not aim at teaching the meaning of love, for that is beyond what can be taught. It does aim, however, at removing the blocks to the awareness of love's presence, which is your natural inheritance. The opposite of love is fear, but what is all encompassing can have no opposite.

The teachings in this book took me to the holiest of holy places inside of me and it was as though I had stepped into a transformation tank or a time tunnel and something so all encompassing and ancient took over my being and my full spiritual vision was installed. I had new software! Everything now had new meaning and everything looked different. I could see the energies beneath that which we see with our shallow ego vision. I felt as though I was really and truly myself in this place. this was the eternal me. I loved this place and I never let go of it again.

My intuitive abilities and inner peace had reached a level that I had never yet experienced in this life and while it was surreal, it also felt so right and so natural. Answers now came quickly and I was like a child with a new toy. I realized that every day presented me with new horizons and that I was being led back to my fully realized self: step-by-step, day-by-day. I could feel the stream of energy go out before me and lead me to the next destination with new insights every day.

This is a good example of how asking or prayer will lead us and guide us and also how the creative works of another human being can serve as such a lifesaver. I have heard people say that it is not possible for one human to learn from another, but that just depends on whether or not we are teachable. We are all so integral and everybody has a book to write - once they know their story.

The teachings and restoration that I underwent during my acceleration were divinely guided and of course, the proof is in the pudding. In the early nineties, I had my aura picture taken during a bookstore spirit fair, by a woman who owned a Kirlian camera. This is a camera that picks up the color or vibration of the energy of the subject it is focused on. The camera produced a Polaroid picture as well as a computer printout. As the printout was coming out of her computer, she was exclaiming, "Oh my God, I have never seen this before. Your aura is all ultraviolet light!" This means that, at least at that moment, everything that I was, both physical and spiritual was in the state of pure consciousness. In this state, we are in full communication with the divine. Christ Consciousness produces this state of clarity and pure bliss.

It is important to mention this because, having experienced the freedom of this level of consciousness, I am able to help others achieve it as well. Just recently in 2014, I had another aura picture taken and this camera showed me as having an all white aura. I have maintained this disposition for two decades, although admittedly, I have had my days. Depending on the equipment used and the sensitivity thereof, white and ultra violet would be closely related if not the same. It is possible to stay in this state, yet is can be challenging when surrounded by human drama.

This state gives me a clear perspective and I am able to see the heart of individuals and am able to ask the masters questions and hear the answers because I am vibrating high enough to be tuned into them.

As time went on, the spirits that once haunted me as a child were no longer scary as I learned that I can set boundries for rmy sensitivity. I began doing readings for other people and learned about the Akashic records, which is the band of consciousness that holds all of the historical information of the physical unfolding of humanity and the planet. It is accessed through our heart chakras and the history is imprinted therein. Do you realize that you are carrying around your very own copy of your soul history in the electromagnetic data of your chakras?

The information I received via these channels was astonishing, clear and accurate – cutting to the quick and allowing my clients to get clarity on things that they were previously confused by. I also received information regarding the mind-body connection to their illnesses and how their history related to physical symptoms. The assistance of the other side or the invisible is there to serve us and make life easier. My earlier experiences were simply demonstrations of the power and connectedness of the subtle realms.

During the years that I was doing many readings, I discovered that everybody goes through the same process that I had been going through, simply at a different pace and often without the knowledge that I had. This is what *A Course in Miracles* refers to as the curriculum. We get stuck in one place and feel like we are going in circles unless we know how to resolve the karma that is holding us back.

When we are able to review the evolution of an individual soul and tap into its goals and history, we can then make the necessary changes and heal what needs to be healed in a very personalized, specific way. There are laws of metaphysics operating at all times, yet most people do not know how to tap into them. Trained intuitives will turn this world around in a way that psychiatry may never do.

Working to find peace amidst the turmoil has been a constant process. I have never opted to use alcohol or drugs to cope. Once I asked my guides when this turbulence around me would end, and the answer I heard was, "When you no longer see it as difficulty." I came to realize that the discordant energies around me forced me inward with a focus that grew in a slow but positive manner until I the awareness of my spirit became brighter and stronger than the outer forces.

Peeling back the layers of my ego was a long process, and building my spirit has been the most rewarding thing I have ever done. There is not a retirement plan, job title or fancy car that can replace feeling good inside and outside.

I want to share everything I have learned because I believe in the humanity's ability to overcome and achieve. I believe in personal responsibility and perseverance and further resolve that if enough people embrace their path, we will find our way out of the seeming financial crisis and many other problems that we are experiencing. gr

To Know Thy Self is to
Know Heaven

Jesus said, "If those who lead you say to you,

'See, the kingdom is in heaven,'

then the birds of heaven will precede you.

If they say to you, '

It is in the sea,'

then the fish will precede you.

But the kingdom is inside of you.

And it is outside of you.

"When you become acquainted with yourselves,

then you will be recognized.

And you will understand that it is you

who are children of the living father.

But if you do not become

acquainted with yourselves,

then you are in poverty, and it is you

who are the poverty."

Journaling Space

Made in the USA
San Bernardino, CA
16 September 2016